GustoNoosa2

GustoNoosa2

Authors	Nathan Hall and Kay Callander
Food Stylist	Hayley Robinson
Photography	Phill Jackson
	Additional photography Alan Jones and Brad Ferguson
Book Design	Kirk Palmer Design
Printer	Geon Group, Australia
Publisher	Visionary Press
	PO Box 2077
	Noosa Heads QLD 4567 Australia
Telephone	+61 7 54480682
Facsimile	+61 7 54735482
Email	info@visionarypress.com

This publication is copyright. Other than for the purposes of and subject to the conditions prescribed under the copyright act, no part of it may be in any form or by any means (electronic, mechanical, mircocopying, photocopying, recording or otherwise) be reproduced, stored in a retrieval system or transmitted without prior written permission. Inquiries should be addressed to the Publisher.

Whilst every care has been taken in the production of this publication, the authors and publisher accept no responsibility for the information contained herein.

© Copyright 2010 Nathan Hall and Kay Callander

ISBN 0 9585660 4 6

GustoNoosa2

Nathan Hall and Kay Callander

Photography Phill Jackson

VISIONARY PRESS

Many people make Gusto a successful restaurant. We would be absolutely nowhere without our staff. Since we opened Gusto many key members of staff have helped us ensure success and have treated the restaurant as their own. Our initial team, some of whom are still with us, strived for the same success we were seeking and we couldn't have done it without their skill or sense of humour. Our current team continues to maintain our high standards and improve our quality. Thank you to each and every one of you.

Thanks to all our fantastic suppliers, the list of which is endless, who put up with our requests and deliver their best produce to our door as many as four times as day.

Writing a book isn't easy and we couldn't have done it without the help of our publisher Judy Vulker who believed in us and repeatedly gave us pointers along the way.

Thanks so much to photographer Phill Jackson for his patience, calmness and creativity. We are lucky to have such a brilliant international photographer living on the Sunshine Coast.

Food stylist Hayley Robinson, thank you for being such a perfectionist. Thank goodness you didn't listen to any of our ideas on food styling – the book wouldn't have been half as good without you.

Mitch Bodycote, our Head Chef, has been with us for over 8 years. Thank you Mitch for your enthusiasm, support, professionalism and incredible energy in the kitchen.

Thank you to Jeroo Pavri from 'The Cooking Company' in Noosa for assisting us with props for the photo shoot from her wonderful shop.

On a personal note thanks to our families who have always encouraged us in whatever path we choose and for instilling into us the love for fine food and wine.

Finally thanks to our regular customers who come to eat at Gusto. We have a huge regular following of customers who have supported us since day one.

Nathan Hall and Kay Callander, November 2010

Noosa main beach is a playground for everyone. Swim, surf, paddleboard, make sandcastles, play beach cricket, or just contemplate the beautiful vista looking from the boardwalk to the north shore. Kay

contents

8 the Gusto story

19 starters

63 mains

97 desserts

120 Gusto basics

124 index

the Gusto story

Well, here we have our second book, which has been a long time in the making. Let me tell you, there's a lot of work involved in writing a book especially when running a busy restaurant and bringing up a young family at the same time. Most of our recipes either live in Nathan's head or are scrawled down in an old notebook – so, documenting recipes that everyone can understand and prepare in a home kitchen takes time. But phew, we did it and we hope you enjoy it.

This book is similar in format to the first edition of Gusto Noosa but contains new recipes with the exception of a couple of old favourites, for which our customers often ask. The recipes are simple and easy to prepare in a home kitchen. We have also included some new and beautiful photos of our favourite Noosa locations which inspire our food.

Its seven years since the publication of our last book and 11 years since opening Gusto. In 2009 we cherished the arrival of our beautiful little boy Jack and I took a side step from the restaurant for my new job as Mum. Jack has transformed our lives and made us realise what a wonderful place Noosa is to have a great business and raise a family. Early mornings are spent daily on Noosa main beach building sand castles and splashing in the waves. Sleeping in after a late night at the restaurant is no longer possible as Jack rises at 5.30am.

People ask how we have managed to run such a successful business for so long. Well, our philosophy is the still same since we started:

- we serve the sort of food that complements the Noosa lifestyle. We want our customers to read the menu and say: 'Wow, I don't know what to choose because everything sounds so damn good',
- we want service to be fast, friendly, unobtrusive and unpretentious,
- consistency, consistency, consistency. A dish has to be the same from one day to the next,
- our food is fresh, clean, sharp, and we use the best ingredients we can source,
- we are hands on and lead by example.

Our philosophy can be challenging and a really hard thing to achieve as Gusto is open 7 days a week. We rely strongly on a faithful team of chefs and waiters who share the same standards and love for their work as we do. Longevity of staff is important and we are very fortunate our team have been with us for many years. Customers return year after year to be greeted by the same waiter which is so special. We might do something as simple as remember their favourite table or the wine they enjoyed the last time they dined. This is something that can only be achieved by retaining long term professional staff.

The food at Gusto is influenced by the Noosa climate, available local produce and of course our own dining experiences. We are lucky in Noosa to be supplied with an abundance of high quality fresh seafood, meat and vegetables. We buy locally as much as possible; prawns from Mooloolaba, scallops from Hervey Bay and strawberries from Eumundi. However, if an ingredient is better from further afield, then we will source it, such as the oysters which come from Coffin Bay in South Australia. We receive 10 dozen oysters every morning at 11.30am and they are always sold out by 8.00pm that same day. Oysters are opened to order and are definitely the best oysters we've ever eaten.

Ideas for new dishes come from our yearly travels to London and Europe. Eating out in other restaurants, especially in different countries always provides a fresh inspiration and we are lucky enough to be able to take a month off annually and travel to the UK to visit family and usually a side trip to one European country. Our inspiration rarely comes from flashy, award winning restaurants but from what we term as 'real' restaurants that serve palatable food. We're definitely not into molecular gastronomy; you'll never get savoury ice cream or dry ice smoking round your plate and definitely no grub in a test tube at Gusto! We serve simple, no fuss, tasty food. Kay

Kay Callander

Nathan and I first saw the Gusto restaurant site when it was under construction in mid 1999. To be honest, we really hadn't thought about opening a restaurant at this point in our lives (we had only met each other 6 months earlier) but as I said at the time 'that doesn't look like a bad spot for a restaurant' and the rest is history. We were both 28 at the time and ready for a challenge.

Our advice to anyone thinking of opening a restaurant is to do it when you are young. Running a restaurant is both mentally and physically exhausting and if you haven't got the stamina forget it! One other vital attribute required is a thick skin. Owning a restaurant is very unforgiving. Everyone has an opinion and one plate of food that impresses one person may not impress the other. We do what we do, believe in it and stick to it!

Nathan and I met in Noosa whilst we were both working in restaurants. I first arrived in Noosa in 1994 as a backpacker from Scotland. During my travels I worked at Coco's at the Noosa National Park in Little Cove. I didn't realise at the time that I would return for a 6 year stint at Coco's but you never know what the future holds.

I loved the place. The restaurant style was so different from what I was used to in Scotland. It was modern, fun and fast with no starchy formalities. I started work at 7.30am and would be done by 4.30pm. It was a dream job. After work I would jog through the beautiful National Park along the coastal track to Hell's Gates and around the Tanglewood track dodging brush turkeys and laughing with the kookaburras. I finished the run with a dip in the ocean at Little Cove. I was fit, healthy, loved my job and was working in paradise.

Later, I worked for Gary Skelton at Season when it was located upstairs above the surf shop in Hastings Street. Season taught me what 'Noosa style' food was all about. Season was a buzz! It was packed to the rafters every night and there was never a dull moment – I loved it.

So, with a solid background in the restaurant game, local market knowledge, and a canny Scottish business brain, Nathan and I signed a lease to our first restaurant. The name Gusto comes from the English meaning 'to perform a task with great zest and passion'. 11 years later we're still at it!

Service with a smile. Monday lunch at Gusto. Paul and I having a laugh. No starchy service or over the top formalities here! Kay

Nathan Hall

Becoming a chef wasn't my childhood dream, it just happened along the way. I left school and like so many other chefs, just fell into the industry. I really didn't have a clue as to what I wanted to do. Basically, I needed a job! My first job in a kitchen was a huge shock to the system and I soon realised that being a chef is a recipe of hard work, determination and more hard work. I also realised fairly quickly that if I was going to be any good at this job I had to learn from the best. I was lucky enough to complete my apprenticeship in some of the best kitchens in Melbourne at the time, including Walter's Wine Bar, Roberto's and Joe's Garage where I learnt the hard yards and discipline as a chef.

Then I packed my bags and headed for London for the next 3 years. Again I was hungry to learn. I worked at Sonny's, Coast, and the most enjoyable of all at St. John with Fergus Henderson. Working with Fergus was an absolute eye opener. Fergus is an extrovert of the best kind. One day we were making rabbit sausages and discussing which herbs to use. Fergus suggested we imagine the rabbit running through a herb garden, picking its own herbs and

We serve the sort of food that people want to eat. Who can resist Roast Bangalow pork with crackling and apple sauce? Nathan

told us to think about what herbs the rabbit would choose. He has a great imagination and this was an entirely new way of thinking for me. I realised how lucky I was to be working with such a creative chef. Together we cooked things I would never have dreamt of cooking back home – tripe, blood cakes with fried eggs, and boiled pig's head. This food was a revelation and the flavours incredible. It was definitely here at St. John that I learnt the simplicity of food and the importance of restraint. Every time we are in London we eat at St. John or St. John Bread and Wine. It is, in my opinion what real food is all about. It's not flashy but it's still voted as one of the world's top 50 restaurants.

Cooking in London was exhausting, even more so than running my own restaurant but the experience was invaluable and I would recommend it to any young chef.

On returning to Australia, as fate would have it I took my first Head Chef's job in Noosa at a brand new restaurant called Riva owned by Nicolas Romer who also owned Coco's. Here I met Kay; we grew closer and on a whim decided to open a restaurant. She's already explained the rest – what's new? She does the talking and I do the cooking, perhaps that's how it still works 11 years on.

Nick, Mitch and I feeling the pressure! Saturday night service – 100 covers, all between 6.00 and 8.00pm. Nathan

For a great way to see the Noosa River, jump on board the Noosa Ferry at Noosa Harbour in Tewantin or at the Sheraton Hotel in Hastings Street. You can get off at a number of stops, have lunch or a coffee then hop back on. Alternatively you can hire a boat, take a picnic and go explore. Kay

the river

starters

This is the largest chapter in the book, simply because starters are our favourite food. Gusto is located adjacent to the stunning Noosa River and our wonderful warm climate dictates the light, fresh nature of our starters. Most of the dishes are suitable for sharing and can either be served individually or on large plates placed in the middle of the table. Kay

20 Bangalow pork and pistachio terrine with prunes and watercress

23 BBQ octopus, pepper mousse, gremolata

24 Pancetta wrapped figs with goats curd and walnut dressing

25 Salmon ceviche

26 Beef carpaccio, anchovy and almond dressing

27 Salt cod brandade with grilled ciabatta, pear and watercress salad

29 Crab cakes, pea, fennel and feta salad

30 Oysters with watermelon salsa and fresh lime

32 Garfish wrapped in vine leaves with salsa verde

35 Baby gem, blue cheese and walnut salad

36 Duck spring rolls

37 Greek salad

38 Gusto meat board with peach chutney

41 Steamed asparagus, fried duck egg, mustard and caper mayonnaise

42 Prawn and garlic bruschetta

44 Salmon gravalax, potato, caper and red onion salad

46 Serrano ham, char grilled peach and blue cheese salad, pedro ximenez dressing

48 Fish chowder

49 Warm smoked trout with pickled cucumber and potato salad

50 Warm beef salad, crispy potato cake, baby gem and walnut salad, mustard dressing

51 Steamed green beans, feta and dukkah

52 Tempura battered stuffed zucchini flowers

55 Tuna tartare, avocado puree

57 Warm broad bean, fennel and feta tart

58 Warm smoked mackerel tart, lyonnaise sauce

starters

Bangalow pork and pistachio terrine with prunes and watercress
Serves 12 as a starter or light lunch

750g Bangalow pork shoulder, diced
750g Bangalow pork belly, diced
15 rashers bacon
1 onion, diced finely
8 cloves garlic, crushed
2 tablespoons finely chopped thyme
1 tablespoon finely chopped sage
50ml brandy
100ml cream
100g shelled pistachio nuts
500ml unsweetened apple juice, reduced to 100ml and cooled
sea salt
freshly ground black pepper
2 bay leaves
2 tea bags
1 small bag pitted prunes
1 large ciabatta loaf
3 bunches watercress

Preheat oven to 200°C.

Mince the pork shoulder, pork belly, 3 rashers of the bacon, onion, garlic, thyme and sage using the coarse mincing attachment of your mincer. Split this mixture in half and put half of it back through the mixer this time using the fine mincing attachment.

In a mixing bowl combine the two textures back together again, add the brandy, cream, pistachio nuts, reduced apple juice and season with sea salt and pepper.

Line a terrine mould or loaf tin with bacon (you will need approximately 12 rashers) placing the rashers length ways across the mould, overlapping each rasher slightly.

Press the mixture firmly into the mould ensuring that the mix reaches all the corners. Fold the bacon that is hanging over the side of the mould on top of the terrine to create a lid. Push a couple of bay leaves on top of the bacon lid.

Bake in a water bath for approximately 1¾ hours to 2 hours. The terrine is cooked when it is firm to touch. Remove from water bath, remove bay leaves, cool and refrigerate overnight before serving.

In a large jug infuse tea bags in boiling water for 5 minutes. Remove tea bags and soak the prunes overnight.

When ready to serve slice the terrine into 1–1½ cm slices. Strain the prunes, grill some ciabatta and arrange neatly on serving plates with watercress.

starters

BBQ octopus, pepper mousse, gremolata
Serves 6 as a starter

Pepper mousse
6 red peppers
1½ leaves gelatine
50ml boiling water
175ml cream
sea salt
freshly ground black pepper
tabasco

Octopus
2 litres court bouillon,
    see Gusto Basics page 122
1kg octopus tentacles
extra virgin olive oil
sea salt
freshly ground black pepper

Gremolata
(makes about 4 tablespoons)
1 lemon grated
3 cloves garlic, crushed
4 tablespoons chopped Italian
    flat leaf parsley

Pepper mousse

Grill peppers until the skins are blackened and place in covered bowl for ½ hour or until cool. This helps the skin come away and the peppers to soften. Rub the peppers to remove skin and seeds then blitz the peppers until smooth in a food processor.

In a saucepan, melt the gelatine in boiling water with one quarter of the pureed peppers.

In a mixer whip the cream until soft peaks form.

Add the remaining pureed peppers with the gelatine mix and gently fold in the cream. Season with sea salt, pepper and a couple of dashes of tabasco. Refrigerate for at least 3 hours before serving.

Octopus

In a saucepan bring the court bouillon up to a gentle simmer and add the octopus. Simmer for 45 minutes.

Remove from the court bouillon and allow to cool. Clean away any sinew on the octopus with a sharp knife and cut each tentacle away from the body. The octopus tentacles can be refrigerated before use.

Preheat a BBQ or char grill, getting it as hot as you can. Brush each octopus tentacle with olive oil and season with sea salt and pepper. Place on char grill and cook for 1 minute on either side, making sure you get some nice char grill marks.

Gremolata

Mix all ingredients together in a bowl.

Remove octopus tentacles from BBQ and place in a mixing bowl. Toss with gremolata and a generous dash of olive oil.

Serve with a spoonful of pepper mousse on the side.

starters

Pancetta wrapped figs with goats curd and walnut dressing
Serves 4 as a starter or light lunch

12 fresh figs
12 slices pancetta
400g fresh goats curd

Walnut dressing
200g walnuts, crushed
½ bunch coriander
1 small red onion, finely diced
½ red chilli, de-seeded finely diced
1 lemon
50ml olive oil

Preheat oven to 180°C

Score the tops of the figs into quarters without completely cutting through.

Wrap each fig with a slice of pancetta and cook for 5 minutes or until the pancetta is crispy and the figs are warm throughout.

While the figs are cooking put the walnuts, coriander, onion and chilli into a bowl. Squeeze the lemon and add to the walnut mix with olive oil and combine.

To serve, place a spoonful of dressing in the centre of the plate. On top of the dressing put 3 scoops of goats curd with a warm fig on top. Sprinkle with salt and pepper and a drizzle of olive oil.

Note: It is important to get the best quality goats curd you can find because it makes the dish extra special. At Gusto we use Woodside goat's curd. Nathan

Salmon ceviche

Serves 4 as a starter

400g salmon, super fresh
8 black Californian dried figs
1 medium red chilli
½ red onion
1 lime, juiced
1 teaspoon sumac
3 cloves garlic, crushed
4 tablespoons, crushed walnuts
2 tablespoons walnut oil
2 teaspoons fresh dill, roughly chopped
pinch sea salt
freshly ground black pepper
lime for serving

Cut the salmon into small cubes, approximately 2cms square. Thinly slice the figs and finely dice the chilli and onion. In a mixing bowl combine all ingredients together.

Taste and adjust seasoning if necessary, add more lime juice if required.

Serve with a wedge of lime.

starters

Beef carpaccio, anchovy and almond dressing
Serves 6 as a starter

Anchovy and almond dressing
3 egg yolks
½ tablespoon Dijon mustard
20g anchovies
2 tablespoons lemon juice
75g crushed almonds
300ml olive oil
pinch sea salt
freshly ground black pepper
hot water for thinning dressing

1kg piece of Wagu beef fillet, frozen before slicing
100g wild rocket leaves
extra virgin olive oil for drizzling
sea salt
2 tablespoons baby capers, washed
wedge of parmesan for shaving
1 large lemon, cut into small wedges

Anchovy and almond dressing
Place egg yolks in a food processor and combine with Dijon mustard, add anchovies, lemon juice and crushed almonds and combine until a smooth consistency. Slowly, add the olive oil, being careful not to split the dressing. Keep adding the olive oil until the mixture is smooth and like mayonnaise in appearance. Season with sea salt and pepper. The dressing may be a bit thick, if so thin it down a little by adding a small amount of boiling water. Place dressing in a squeeze bottle and store in the fridge until required.

Wrap beef fillet tightly in plastic wrap and place in freezer for at least 6 hours before use.

Using a very sharp knife, slice the beef as thinly as you can. Alternatively, use a meat slicer if you have one. Allow approximately 8 slices per person, depending on the size of the beef fillet.

Place a few rocket leaves around the base of serving plate and drizzle lightly with olive oil and season with sea salt.

Place the slices of beef on top of the rocket and sprinkle with a few capers.

Drizzle lightly with olive oil and zig zag the anchovy and almond dressing across the top. Shave parmesan around and about. Season the beef with sea salt and serve with a small wedge of lemon.

Salt cod brandade with grilled ciabatta, pear and watercress salad
Serves 6 as a starter

400g salt cod
1 clove garlic, crushed
150g desiree potatoes, diced and boiled until soft
100ml milk
100ml olive oil
1 ciabatta loaf
2 hard pears, thinly sliced
2 bunches of watercress

Soak the cod in a basin of cold water in the refrigerator for at least 24 hours. Replace the water and rinse the cod every 6 hours.

Bring a pot of water up to a gentle simmer and poach the cod until its flesh becomes flaky. Remove from the water and remove skin and bones.

Heat a large saucepan then add a dash of olive oil and gently cook the garlic. Then add to the saucepan the cod and cooked potato. Whilst stirring, add the milk and olive oil separately a little at a time. Stir until the potato breaks up and ingredients are incorporated then remove from heat. Cool and refrigerate.

Serve the brandade on some grilled ciabatta with a little pear and watercress salad on the side. Drizzle the watercress with olive oil.

starters

Crab cakes, pea, fennel and feta salad
Serves 4 as a starter

Crab cakes
250g crab meat, cooked
250g cooked desiree potatoes (mashed)
sea salt
2 eggs for egg wash
100ml milk for egg wash
250g breadcrumbs
1 litre vegetable oil for deep frying

Pea, fennel and feta salad
1 small fennel bulb
50ml extra virgin olive oil
dash lemon juice
300g fresh peas, blanched with half bunch fresh mint
¼ bunch fresh mint, picked
sea salt
120g feta

Crab cakes

In a bowl combine the crab meat, mashed potato and a pinch of sea salt.

Divide the mixture into 12 so you have 3 crab cakes per person. Then mould together with your hands into small oval shaped cakes, keeping them all a uniform shape and size.

Whisk together the milk and egg with a fork and coat each crab cake lightly with egg wash, then roll in breadcrumbs. The crab cakes are now ready for deep frying. Refrigerate until ready to fry.

Pea, fennel and feta salad

Using a mandolin, slice the fennel bulb very finely. If you haven't got a mandolin use a sharp knife, slicing it as thinly as you can. Place the fennel in a bowl with the olive oil and a dash of lemon juice, add the peas and picked mint leaves. Season with sea salt.

Break up the feta and add to the salad.

Heat the vegetable oil in a large saucepan to 180°C, or heat a deep fryer if you have one.

Gently drop each crab cake into the hot oil and cook until light golden brown. Remove with a slotted spoon and drain on kitchen paper.

To serve, spoon a little of the salad on individual serving plates and place the crab cakes on top, allowing 3 per person.

starters

Oysters with watermelon salsa and fresh lime
Serves 4 as a starter

200g seedless watermelon
2 dozen best quality oysters
2 fresh limes
1 red onion, finely diced
100ml raspberry vinegar
crushed ice for serving

Remove the skin of the watermelon and dice very finely. Mix with the diced onion and raspberry vinegar. Refrigerate until required.

Open the oysters with an oyster knife just before serving, being careful to retain all the juice inside the shell. Do not wash the oyster as this washes away all the lovely salty flavour.

Serve oysters on top of crushed ice. Place a small ramekin of salsa on the side and finish off with half a fresh lime.

Note: We have included this recipe for watermelon salsa which was also in our first book as it is incredibly popular. We sell dozens and dozens of oysters this way in the restaurant and nearly everyone who tries them for the first time asks what's in the salsa. Of course the secret ingredient here is the raspberry vinegar. Nathan

starters

Garfish wrapped in vine leaves with salsa verde
Serves 4 as a starter

Garfish
8 garfish fillets
1 packet of vine leaves (500g)
2 lemons
Sea salt
Freshly ground black pepper

Filling
300g kipfler potatoes
2 tablespoons Italian flat leaf parsley, finely chopped
1 small red onion, finely sliced
2 tablespoons baby capers, washed
3 tablespoons green olives, pitted and sliced
1 tablespoon sherry vinegar
2 cloves garlic, crushed

4 tablespoons salsa verde, see Gusto Basics page 123

Preheat oven to 250°C

Garfish
Prepare garfish by removing any bones and rinse vine leaves under cold running water and set aside.

Filling
To make the filling, cook the potatoes in boiling salted water for approximately 20 minutes or until soft, then peel and finely slice into thin rounds and place in a mixing bowl. Add all other ingredients and season with sea salt and black pepper.

To wrap the garfish, lay out a vine leaf on a work bench and lay a garfish fillet skin side down on top of the vine leaf. Place a tablespoonful of the filling along the garfish fillet and then place another garfish fillet on top of the filling. Roll the vine leaf around the garfish in a cigar like fashion.

To cook, place the wrapped garfish on an oiled baking tray and bake for 5 minutes at 250°C.

Serve with a generous spoonful of room temperature salsa verde and half a lemon.

Note: The picture shows whole garfish, the recipe uses fillets as it's easier for home cooking as all the bones are removed. You can use whole fish but be warned, the bones can be fiddly and difficult to remove. Nathan

Baby gem, blue cheese and walnut salad

Serves 6 as a side

50g gorgonzola
150g mascarpone
100ml cream
3 baby gem lettuces, washed
100g walnuts
garlic dressing, see Gusto Basics page 121
sea salt

Preheat oven to 180°C.

With your hands roughly break up the gorgonzola and place in a mixing bowl. Add the mascarpone and combine gently with a fork. Do not stir vigorously. Stir the cream in slowly until it is a nice smooth texture. Refrigerate until required.

Place the walnuts on a tray and toast in the oven for 5 minutes. Remove and scatter in a clean towel and rub gently to remove the skins.

Remove outer leaves of lettuce, using only the crispy hearts. Separate the leaves and place in a mixing bowl with the walnuts. Add a generous amount of dressing and toss through, making sure each leaf gets lightly coated. Transfer to a clean serving bowl. Take the cheese from the fridge and using a teaspoon, spoon small amounts throughout the salad and season with sea salt.

starters

Duck spring rolls
Serves 6 as a starter

1kg duck fat
6 large duck legs
1 bunch spring onions, washed and finely chopped
250g bean shoots
3 tablespoons dukkah, see Gusto Basics page 120
150ml honey soy, see Gusto Basics page 121
Sea salt
Freshly ground black pepper
1 packet spring roll pastry wrappers, 25cm x 25cm
1 litre vegetable oil for deep frying

Preheat oven to 180°C.

Place the duck legs in a large roasting tray skin side up and cover with duck fat. Cover in aluminium foil and place in oven for 1–1½ hours or until the meat falls from the bone.

When the duck is ready, remove from the fat using tongs and place on a wire rack in a clean roasting tray. Return to the oven for a few minutes until the skin is crispy. Remove from oven and set aside until cool enough to handle. The duck fat can be cooled, refrigerated and reused.

Remove meat from the bones and roughly shred.

In a large mixing bowl place the duck meat, spring onions and bean shoots. Add 2 tablespoons of the dukkah (reserve 1 tablespoon for serving), 100ml of the honey soy (reserve 50ml for dipping sauce) and season with sea salt and pepper. Mix until all ingredients are incorporated.

Lay out the spring roll wrappers on work bench and place a generous tablespoonful of mix diagonally across each wrapper. Lift the bottom corner up over the mix and tuck it in tightly so you have a cigar shape. Now tightly fold in left and right corners meeting in the middle and continue to roll applying pressure as you do so. Brush a little water on top corner to stick the wrappers together. Continue until you have used all the filling.

Heat the vegetable oil in a large saucepan to 180°C or use a deep fat fryer if you have one. Gently place each spring roll into the hot oil and cook until golden brown. Do not fry any more than 6 at one time. Remove with tongs and drain on kitchen paper.

Pile the spring rolls on top of each other on a large service plate with a ramekin of honey soy on the side. Sprinkle with dukkah and serve in the middle of the table.

Greek salad

Serves 4 as a side

4 large vine tomatoes (blanched and skin removed), thick sliced
150g mixed good quality olives
1 red onion, sliced
1 small cucumber, seeds removed, cut into 8cm batons
small handful Italian flat leaf parsley, roughly picked
extra virgin olive oil
juice of 1 small lemon
sea salt
freshly ground black pepper
½ teaspoon sumac
200g Persian feta

In a large mixing bowl place, tomatoes, olives, red onion, cucumber and parsley.

Add a generous dash of olive oil, lemon juice, sea salt and pepper. With your hands gently toss all ingredients around bowl, making sure everything gets nicely coated in dressing. Add more olive oil if required. Add the sumac, a little at a time, tasting as you go, it should taste really fresh and tangy.

Roughly break up the feta into cubes and disperse generously throughout the salad. Serve in a large bowl.

starters

Gusto meat board with peach chutney
Serves 4 as a starter or light lunch

Peach chutney
4 fresh peaches, pitted and diced
150ml raspberry vinegar
200g castor sugar
1 red onion, finely diced

Meat board
8 slices Serrano ham
16 slices beef salami
12 slices chorizo sausage
24 large green Sicilian olives
1 ciabatta loaf

Peach chutney
Place all ingredients in a saucepan, bring to a gentle boil and simmer for 10 minutes. Remove from heat, cool and refrigerate until required. The chutney keeps for 7 days in a refrigerator.

To serve, use a wooden chopping board, placing the meat slices side by side. Dot the olives around the board and serve the peach chutney in a ramekin. Serve with grilled ciabatta.

Note: You can either serve this on small individual chopping boards for each person, as in the photograph opposite or on one big board and place in the middle of the table for sharing. Perfect for pre-dinner drinks. Kay

starters

Steamed asparagus, fried duck egg, mustard and caper mayonnaise

Serves 4 as a starter

2 bunches asparagus
4 duck eggs
extra virgin olive oil
mustard and caper mayonnaise, see Gusto Basics page 121
sea salt
freshly ground black pepper
bunch of watercress, washed
1 tablespoon dukkah, see Gusto Basics page 120

Boil a saucepan of water and steam asparagus for approximately 1 to 2 minutes until 'al dente'.

Whilst asparagus is cooking, gently fry duck eggs in a little olive oil.

Spread some mustard and caper mayonnaise on serving plates and lay asparagus over the top, season with sea salt and pepper and drizzle lightly with olive oil.

Place a fried egg on top of asparagus.

Garnish each plate with a few sprigs of watercress and a sprinkle of dukkah.

starters

Prawn and garlic bruschetta
Serves 4 as a starter

extra virgin olive oil
12 large king prawns, shelled and de-veined, heads and tails left on
100g unsalted butter, diced
4 cloves of garlic, sliced finely
sea salt
freshly ground black pepper
4 tablespoons Italian flat leaf parsley, roughly chopped
8 slices ciabatta bread, cut thickly
2 lemons for serving

Preheat oven to 200°C.

Heat a large thick based, oven proof frying pan.

Add a good dash of olive oil to the pan and when it is very hot seal the prawns on either side until they start to colour slightly.

Transfer pan to a hot oven for approximately 3–5 minutes, depending on the size of the prawns. The prawns are ready when they are pink in colour and slightly firm to touch.

Remove the pan from the oven and return to stove top, finish by adding butter and garlic. Be careful not to burn the garlic. Season with sea salt and pepper and stir through parsley.

Meanwhile brush the sliced ciabatta with olive oil and char grill slices until golden brown on each side.

To serve, arrange the prawns (allowing 3 per person) on serving plates, spooning the garlic and oil over the top, serve the ciabatta (allowing 2 slices per serve) to the side of the prawns with a lemon cheek.

starters

Salmon gravalax, potato, caper and red onion salad
Serves 6–8 as a starter

Curing

750g brown sugar
750g sea salt
1 bunch dill, roughly chopped
1 side Atlantic salmon. Ask the fish monger to remove skin and bones

Salad

8 kipfler potatoes, peeled
2 tablespoons baby capers, washed to remove saltiness
1 red onion, sliced
1 tablespoons dill, finely chopped
2 tablespoons seeded mustard mayonnaise, see Gusto Basics Basics page 121
1 bunch watercress
extra virgin olive oil
sea salt

To cure the salmon

Mix together the sugar, salt and dill. Place the whole side of salmon in a large flat tray and cover completely with the mixture. Cover the tray with plastic wrap. Leave overnight or for 12 hours.

Remove salmon from curing mixture and wash well under cold water. Pat dry, with a clean tea towel.

Using a flexible filleting knife, slice the salmon as thinly as you like it and refrigerate until ready to serve.

Salad

Cook the potatoes in boiling salted water and cut into bite sized pieces. Place in a bowl with capers, onion and dill. Dress with a couple of tablespoons of seeded mustard mayonnaise.

To serve, arrange the slices of gravalax neatly on a serving plate, with a spoonful of potato salad on the side. Serve with some watercress, drizzle with olive oil and sprinkle with sea salt.

starters

Serrano ham, char grilled peach and blue cheese salad, pedro ximenez dressing

Serves 4 as a starter

200g rocket leaves
16 slices thin Serrano ham
4 peaches, each cut into 6 segments
extra virgin olive oil
200g good quality blue cheese
sea salt
freshly ground black pepper
4 sprigs of fresh thyme, picked
pedro ximinez dressing see Gusto Basics, page 122

Preheat a char grill.

Place some rocket leaves on the base of serving plates.

Lay the Serrano ham on top of the rocket.

Brush the peach segments lightly with olive oil and char grill for approximately 1 minute on either side until char marks appear. Remove from grill and disperse the peaches on top of the Serrano ham.

Slice cheese and break into small pieces. Evenly distribute cheese over the salad.

Sprinkle a little thyme over each salad and season with sea salt and pepper.

Drizzle each salad generously with pedro ximinez dressing.

starters

Fish chowder

Serves 4 as a starter or light lunch

Base (which can be made beforehand and kept in refrigerator)
150g unsalted butter
1 small onion, finely diced
4 cloves garlic, crushed
150g plain flour
1 litre fish stock,
see Gusto Basics page 121
250ml cream
2 large desiree potatoes, diced into 1 cm cubes
sea salt
freshly ground black pepper

Chowder
1 large leek, washed and cut into 2cm diamonds
200g cleaned prawn meat
200g white flaky fish, roughly cut into 2cm squares
100g cleaned cuttlefish, sinew removed, cut into approximately 3cm strips
12 cooked mussels, removed from shells
4 large scallops
sea salt
freshly ground black pepper
4 tablespoons Italian parsley, roughly chopped
extra virgin olive oil
bread for serving

Base

In a saucepan, melt butter and sweat off the onion and garlic until translucent.

Make a roux, by stirring in the flour with a wooden spoon. Let it cook out for 2 minutes, being careful it doesn't burn.

Gradually add the fish stock, stirring gently. Add the cream and bring slowly up to a gentle simmer.

Add the potato and simmer until soft. Season with sea salt and a little pepper.

This base mixture can now be cooled and refrigerated for up to 2 days before use.

Chowder

In a saucepan gently heat the base mixture to a slow simmer.

Add the leeks and all the seafood, except for the scallops. Gently poach for approximately 3–5 minutes, until seafood is lightly cooked.

Check the seasoning and add parsley.

Meanwhile, heat a frying pan and add a good dash of olive oil. When it is really hot, sear the scallops for 30 seconds on one side only. They should not be cooked all the way through.

Serve the chowder in heated soup bowls and place a scallop in the centre of each bowl, the seared side of the scallop should be presentation side up. Finish by drizzling the soup with a little olive oil.

Warm smoked trout with pickled cucumber and potato salad

Serves 4 as a starter or light lunch

8 small kipfler potatoes, peeled
seed mustard mayonnaise,
   see Gusto Basics page 121
2 whole smoked trout, skin and
   bones removed
cucumber pickle,
   see Gusto Basics page 120
2 bunches watercress
extra virgin olive oil

Preheat oven to 180°C.

Boil the potatoes in salted water until soft. Remove and cut into barrels, approximately 3cm long. In a mixing bowl generously dress the potatoes with seed mustard dressing.

Place the trout fillets skin side down on an oiled tray and warm them in the oven for 3 to 5 minutes.

To serve place a generous amount of cucumber pickle on a plate, with a spoonful of the potatoes to the side and a fillet of trout per person on top of the potatoes. Don't worry if the fillet breaks up a little. Finish with a few watercress leaves and a drizzle of olive oil.

starters

Warm beef salad, crispy potato cake, baby gem and walnut salad, mustard dressing

Serves 4 as a starter or light lunch

4 medium desiree potatoes, peeled
extra virgin olive oil
400g beef fillet, cut into thin strips
1 baby gem lettuce, washed
2 tablespoons baby capers, washed
4 tablespoons walnuts, roughly chopped
2 tablespoons dill, roughly chopped
sea salt
freshly ground black pepper
English mustard mayonnaise, see Gusto Basics page 121

Firstly prepare the potato cake. Preheat oven to 200°C.

Par-boil the potatoes (whole) for 10 minutes in salted water. Remove potatoes from the water and when cool enough to handle grate them on rough edge of grater. Season the potatoes with sea salt and pepper.

Heat 4 small blini pans and add a good dash of olive oil to each (approximately 2 tablespoons). When the oil is really hot add the grated potato, pushing it down into the edges of the pan. Place the pans in the oven and cook for approximately 15 minutes or until the potato is crispy and golden brown.

Heat a frying pan, add a little olive oil and sear the beef strips for a minute on either side keeping them rare.

In a bowl place baby gem leaves, capers, walnuts, dill and beef strips. Dress generously with hot English mustard dressing. Taste and season with sea salt and pepper.

To serve, place the crispy potato cake in the centre of serving plate. Neatly arrange the salad on top, with a drizzle of olive oil.

Steamed green beans, feta and dukkah
Serves 4 as a side dish

400g best quality green beans
extra virgin olive oil
sea salt
freshly ground black pepper
1 tablespoon dukkah, see Gusto Basics page 120
120g goat's milk feta

Steam the green beans in boiling salted water until 'al dente'. Toss generously with a good quality olive oil. Season with sea salt and pepper, sprinkle with dukkah then crumble the feta over the top.

starters

Tempura battered stuffed zucchini flowers
Serves 4 as a starter

Zucchini flowers
200g fresh ricotta
2 eggs
50g Parmesan, finely grated
1 lemon, zest only, finely grated
pinch of sea salt
8 large zucchini flowers

Tempura batter
1 cup flour
1 egg
1 cup iced water

1 litre of vegetable oil for deep frying
Salsa verde for serving, see Gusto Basics page 123

Zucchini flowers

In a mixing bowl, mix together ricotta, eggs, Parmesan, grated lemon zest, pinch salt until well combined.

Lay each zucchini flower flat and gently spoon cheese mixture into the flower. Stuff each flower full, but not overflowing, gently folding flower over to seal it closed. Refrigerate, whilst you prepare batter.

Tempura batter

Whisk together flour, egg and iced water until incorporated.

Heat the vegetable oil in a large saucepan to 180°C, or use a deep fryer if you have one. Dip each zucchini flower lightly in the batter and gently drop into the hot oil and cook until golden brown. Remove with a slotted spoon and drain on absorbent paper.

Serve immediately with a generous spoonful of salsa verde. Perfect on a large platter in the middle of the table.

starters

Tuna tartare, avocado puree
Serves 4 as a starter

Avocado puree
2 ripe avocadoes
tabasco, approximately 6 dashes, depending how hot you like it
50ml extra virgin olive oil
1 lemon, juiced
pinch sea salt
freshly ground black pepper

Tuna tartare
400g sashimi grade yellowfin tuna, cut into 1cm cubes
sea salt
freshly ground black pepper
4 tablespoons sesame oil
2 tablespoons sesame seeds
extra virgin olive oil for drizzling

Avocado puree
Prepare the avocado puree, by blitzing all ingredients in a food processor, except for the lemon juice. Add this last and taste as you do so, adding as much or as little as you like. We like it tangy!

Tuna tartare
Place the diced tuna in a bowl and season with sea salt and pepper, add the sesame oil and stir through.

To serve, arrange tuna neatly in small mound on centre of serving plates and simply spoon a quenelle (using 2 tablespoons) of avocado puree on the side. Sprinkle tuna lightly with sesame seeds. Drizzle lightly with olive oil.

Warm broad bean, fennel and feta tart

Serves 12 as a starter or light lunch

Shortcrust pastry – enough for
1 x 30cm fluted flan tin
165g butter
330g plain flour
pinch salt
40ml iced water

Tart mix
250g unsalted butter
2 fennel bulbs, finely diced
2 onions, finely diced
6 cloves garlic, crushed
500g broad beans, shelled
5 eggs, beaten
4 tablespoons dill, roughly chopped
400ml cream
sea salt,
freshly ground black pepper
200g goats milk feta
2 tablespoons parmesan, grated
mixed green leaves to serve
extra virgin olive oil

Pastry

In a food processor place the butter, flour and salt and pulse until breadcrumb consistency.

Slowly add the water and pulse until the mixture comes together. Wrap in plastic wrap and refrigerate for 1 hour.

Preheat oven to 160°C.

Roll out the pastry, maintaining an even thickness. Roll the pastry on to the back of your rolling pin to pick it up and place into buttered flan tin.

Bake blind by lining the pastry shell with plastic wrap and filling with baking beans. Bake for 10 minutes. Remove plastic wrap and beans. Check that the pastry base is cooked, if not place the tart in the oven without the baking beans for just a couple of minutes to finish cooking the base. Allow to cool and your tart is ready to fill.

Tart mix

Preheat oven to 170°C.

Melt butter in a heavy based frying pan. Sweat off fennel, onion and garlic until translucent and soft without any colour. Strain the butter off and discard.

In a large bowl mix together the cooked fennel, onion and garlic with the broad beans, eggs, dill, cream and season with sea salt and pepper.

Pour the mixture into pastry shell. Break up the feta and dot over the top of the tart. Sprinkle with grated parmesan. Place tart in oven for approximately 45 minutes or until tart is golden brown and set.

Slice and serve warm with a little green leaf salad. Drizzle with olive oil and season with sea salt.

starters

Warm smoked mackerel tart, lyonnaise sauce
Serves 6 as a starter

Shortcrust pastry
This recipe is enough for 6 x 10cm fluted flan tins with removable bases
165g butter, diced and hard
330g plain flour
pinch salt
40ml iced water

Filling
400g desiree potatoes, peeled, boiled and mashed
200ml cream
4 eggs, beaten
2 tablespoons chopped chives
200g smoked mackerel, broken into small pieces
sea salt
freshly ground black pepper

Lyonnaise sauce
150g butter
1 onion, finely diced
½ fennel bulb, finely diced
6 cloves garlic, crushed
75ml cream
1 tablespoon dukkah,
  see Gusto basics page 120

To serve
6 teaspoons crème fraiche

Pastry
In a food processor place the butter, flour and salt and pulse until breadcrumb consistency.

Slowly add the water and pulse until the mixture comes together. Wrap in plastic wrap and refrigerate for 1 hour.

Pre-heat oven to 160°C.

Divide the pastry into 6 and roll to an even thickness in round shapes. Place into flan tins which have been greased lightly with butter and dusted with flour.

Bake blind by lining the pastry shell with plastic wrap and filling with baking beans. Bake for 10 minutes. Remove plastic wrap and beans. Check the bases of the tarts are cooked through. If not, place the tarts back in the oven without the baking beans for 2–3 minutes. Remove from oven, cool and your tart is ready for filling.

Filling
Preheat oven to 170°C.

In a mixing bowl place the warm mashed potato. Mix in the cream and whisk to combine. Add the beaten eggs, chives and mackerel pieces and mix until well combined. Season with sea salt and pepper. Spoon into pastry cases and bake in the oven for 20–25 minutes until they are set and light golden in colour. Carefully remove from flan tins and serve warm.

Lyonnaise sauce
Melt the butter in a frying pan and sweat off the onion, fennel and garlic until soft. Strain and puree in a blender. Add the cream and serve warm with a sprinkle of dukkah.

To serve, place a few tablespoons of lyonnaise sauce in the centre of a plate. Place a tart on top with a small quenelle (using 2 teaspoons) of crème fraiche on top of the tart.

Note: I use plastic wrap for the pastry in the oven, however if you prefer, you can use baking paper. Nathan

mains

As with all our food we try and keep things as simple as possible. Buy the best quality ingredients money can buy and treat them without fuss. We strive to get the basics right like serving food on a hot plate, seasoning things properly and not overcooking them.

We've eaten in top end restaurants in London and Paris where the chef has started with wonderful ingredients and over worked them so much that by the time the food reaches the plate it no longer tastes of the original ingredients. The best thing about good, fresh food is it that doesn't need too much done to it to taste great. Nathan

64 Braised white rabbit

67 BBQ spatchcock, apple and raisin couscous

68 BBQ veal fillets, warm pumpkin, pine nut and goat's feta salad

70 Braised lamb gnocchi, peas, mint, and Jerusalem artichoke chips

73 BBQ octopus and chorizo, braised peppers and chickpeas

74 Grilled eye fillet of beef, potato galette and mushrooms

76 Butternut pumpkin tortellini, cherry tomato, sage butter

79 Half a char grilled baby chicken, warm pea, artichoke and bacon salad

80 Pancetta, garlic, chilli and tomato spaghetti, Woodside goats curd

81 Chorizo, chilli and roast pepper fusilli

82 Crispy skin salmon fillet with mash and pickled cucumber

85 Crispy duck salad with radicchio, beans and prunes

86 Prawn ravioli with leek and lemon butter sauce

88 Roast lamb rack with spinach, lentils and bacon, yoghurt dressing

91 Roast Bangalow pork rack, creamy mash, braised baby gem, walnut, bacon and apple salad

92 Seared tuna spaghetti

92 Bug linguine

mains

Braised white rabbit

Serves 6

2 whole white rabbits, approximately 1.7kg each, cleaned and skinned
extra virgin olive oil
3 onions, peeled and roughly chopped
500ml unsweetened apple juice
500ml dry white wine
500ml cream
200g Dijon mustard
2 cinnamon sticks
4 bay leaves
12 baby field onions
4 tablespoons Italian flat leaf parsley, finely chopped
12 slices pancetta
sea salt
freshly ground black pepper
1 quantity potato mash, see Gusto Basics page 122

Preheat oven to 240°C.

To prepare each rabbit, remove the front and hind legs and then cut the hind legs in half. Cut the saddle into 3 equal parts (you can ask your butcher to do this for you). This will allow 2 pieces of brown meat (legs) and one piece of white meat (saddle) per portion.

In a hot pan, with a little olive oil, seal the rabbit on all sides until the skin is a light golden brown and then remove from heat.

Place roughly chopped onions on the bottom of a heavy based braising dish then sit rabbit on top.

In a separate bowl combine apple juice, wine, cream and Dijon mustard and pour over rabbit. Add cinnamon sticks and bay leaves and cover tightly with aluminium foil. Braise in a hot oven for 45 minutes.

While the rabbit is cooking, peel the baby onions and sauté over a low heat with a little olive oil until the onions are soft and have caramelised, this may take about 25 minutes.

When cooked, take the rabbit out of the braising dish. Strain and discard the chunky bits. Keep the sauce. Put the rabbit and sauce back into a pan, add the caramelised onions and bring to the boil. Taste and adjust seasoning. Turn the heat down and let the rabbit simmer for a further 5 minutes. Just before serving add the chopped parsley.

Cook the pancetta in a frying pan until crispy.

In a separate pot, heat potato mash until it is piping hot. Serve a generous portion of mash to mop up the sauce, evenly distribute the rabbit and sauce between the plates. Place 2 slices of pancetta and 2 onions on each plate.

Note: This dish lends itself perfectly to being prepared the day before and is a knockout winter dish. Nathan

BBQ spatchcock, apple and raisin couscous
Serves 4

Marinade
4 organic #5 spatchcocks, deboned and butterflied
1 lemon, zested
6 cloves garlic, crushed
100ml extra virgin olive oil

100ml orange juice
75g sugar
100g of raisins
250g couscous
250ml boiling water
50g unsalted butter, cubed
sea salt
freshly ground black pepper
1 granny smith apple, thinly sliced
150g baby spinach leaves
2 baby gem lettuces, centre leaves only
½ red onion, sliced
12 slices pancetta
dukkah, see Gusto Basics page 120
garlic dressing, see Gusto Basics page 121

Marinade
Marinate the spatchcocks with the lemon zest, garlic and olive oil. Cover with plastic wrap and refrigerate overnight.

Boil the orange juice and sugar and add the raisins. Leave to simmer for 2 minutes, remove from heat and let sit for approximately 30 minutes or until the raisins are plump.

Drain the liquid and set raisins aside.

Put the couscous in a large bowl and cover with 250ml of boiling water. Add the butter and a good pinch of sea salt and cover with plastic wrap. Leave until all the liquid has been absorbed.

Preheat oven to 240°C and preheat a char grill or BBQ.

Remove spatchcocks from marinade.

Grill skin side down for 3 minutes, making sure you get some really good char marks.

Transfer to oven and cook for approximately 8 minutes until cooked all the way through. Insert a skewer into the thigh bone to ensure spatchcock is properly cooked and no blood appears.

Add the raisins, sliced apple, baby spinach leaves, baby gem leaves and red onion to the couscous and gently mix through with a little olive oil to moisten and season to taste.

Fry the pancetta in a hot frying pan with a little olive oil until crisp, let cool and then cut into small pieces.

To serve, place a generous spoonful of couscous salad in the centre of a plate and drizzle with the garlic dressing then sprinkle with dukkah. Scatter the crispy pancetta on top of the salad. Cut each spatchcock in ½ and serve on top of the salad.

BBQ veal fillets, warm pumpkin, pine nut and goat's feta salad

Serves 4 as a main course

1 kg veal fillet
6 roma tomatoes
sea salt
freshly ground black pepper
extra virgin olive oil
1 butternut pumpkin, peeled, seeds removed
100g pine nuts
100g rocket leaves
120g goat's feta
1 tablespoon dukkah, see Gusto Basics page 120
pedro ximinez dressing, see Gusto Basics page 122

Preheat oven to 180°C.

Firstly prepare the veal. Using a sharp knife cut the fillet into approximately 80g medallions (you can ask your butcher to do this). Cover each medallion in plastic wrap and beat each side with a meat cleaver or heavy based pot if you haven't got a cleaver. Remove plastic wrap and refrigerate until required.

Remove the eyes of the tomatoes and cut in ½ lengthways. Place on a wire rack in a roasting tray, season with sea salt and drizzle with olive oil. Roast for 30 minutes, remove from oven and set aside.

Cut the pumpkin into chunks roughly 5cm square and toss in olive oil. Place on a wire rack in a roasting tray, season with sea salt and cover with aluminium foil. Roast for 45 minutes or until soft. Remove from oven and set aside.

Place the pine nuts in a dry non-stick frying pan and toast for a minute or so on stove top. Be careful not to burn.

Preheat a BBQ or char grill as hot as you can get it. Season the veal with sea salt and pepper and brush with a little olive oil. Grill for approximately 2 minutes on either side, being careful not to overcook. It should still be pink in the middle. Leave to rest for a couple of minutes.

Put the warm pumpkin in a large mixing bowl with the rocket and pine nuts. Season with sea salt and pepper and toss with pedro ximinez dressing. Break up the feta into large chunks and mix through the salad. Sprinkle the salad with dukkah.

To serve, place the roast tomatoes on a plate with a generous amount of warm pumpkin salad, with the veal fillets to the side.

mains

Braised lamb gnocchi, peas, mint, and Jerusalem artichoke chips
Serves 6 as a main course

Lamb
300g carrots, peeled and roughly chopped
300g onions, peeled and roughly chopped
50g leeks, washed and roughly chopped
½ head of garlic, split through middle
6 lamb shanks
3 bay leaves
1 litre chicken stock, see Gusto Basics page 120
50g butter
175g peas, blanched
sea salt
freshly ground black pepper
½ bunch fresh mint

Gnocchi
1 amount of gnocchi, see Gusto Basics page 122 (Note, the gnocchi can be made beforehand and reheated in boiling water before adding to the sauce).

Jerusalem artichoke chips
(fry just before serving)
6 small Jerusalem artichokes
1 litre vegetable oil for deep frying
sea salt

Lamb
Preheat oven to 200°C.

Scatter the carrots, onions, leeks and garlic on the bottom of a large, deep baking tray. Lay the lamb shanks on top with the bay leaves and cover with the stock. Cover with aluminium foil and cook for 2 hours.

Remove the lamb shanks then rip the meat from the bone.

Strain the braising juices and discard the vegetables and bay leaves.

In a pan simmer and reduce the stock by half, then add a couple of knobs of butter and whisk well.

Add the meat and the peas and heat through. Season with sea salt and pepper. Add the cooked gnocchi and stir through. Remove from heat and add torn mint leaves. Serve in bowls with a generous amount of Jerusalem artichoke chips.

Jerusalem artichoke chips
Heat the vegetable oil in a large saucepan or use a deep fryer if you have one. Gently drop the slices of Jerusalem artichoke into the hot oil and cook until golden brown and crispy. They will only take 20-30 seconds. Remove from the oil using a slotted spoon and drain on kitchen paper. Season them with sea salt.

BBQ octopus and chorizo, braised peppers and chickpeas
Serves 4 as a main course

2 litres octopus court bouillon, see Gusto Basics page 122
800g octopus tentacles, cleaned
4 chorizo sausages
sea salt
finely ground black pepper
extra virgin olive oil
300g chickpeas
2 roast peppers, skin off, roughly chopped
2 roast red chillies, skin off, finely diced
2 tablespoons capers, washed
250ml chicken stock, see Gusto Basics page 120
2 tablespoons sherry vinegar
100g butter, cubed
4 tablespoons fresh coriander, chopped
4 slices ciabatta bread for serving

Prepare the octopus by bringing the court bouillon up to a gentle simmer in a saucepan. Add the octopus and cook for 45 minutes.

Remove octopus from the court bouillon and allow to cool. Clean away any sinew on the octopus with a sharp knife and cut each tentacle away from the body. The tentacles can be refrigerated before use.

Preheat a BBQ or char grill, getting it as hot as you can. Slice the chorizo into 2cm slices. Brush the octopus and chorizo with olive oil and season with sea salt and pepper. Place both on the char grill and cook for 1 minute on either side, making sure you get some nice char grill marks. Remove from grill and slice the octopus into bite size pieces.

Preheat a frying pan and add a dash of olive oil. When the oil is hot transfer the octopus and chorizo to the pan. Add the chickpeas, peppers, chilli, capers and chicken stock and bring up to a simmer. Cook for 2 minutes. Add the sherry vinegar and a few knobs of butter to thicken and enrich the sauce. Season with sea salt and pepper. Turn off the heat and add the chopped coriander. Serve immediately with a slice of grilled ciabatta on the side.

mains

Grilled eye fillet of beef, potato galette and mushrooms

Serves 4 as a main course

Potato galette
1 small onion, finely diced
2 tablespoons cooking salt
500ml cream
6 cloves garlic, crushed
3 tablespoons Dijon mustard
1 tablespoon hot English mustard
1 teaspoon thyme, finely chopped
2 bay leaves
150g butter, cubed
sea salt
freshly ground black pepper
6 large desire potatoes, washed and peeled
100g parmesan cheese, grated
greaseproof paper

Beef and mushrooms
4 fillet steaks (200g each)
sea salt
freshly ground black pepper
extra virgin olive oil
150g button mushrooms, quartered
150g oyster mushrooms, sliced
150g shitake mushrooms, sliced
1 teaspoon thyme, finely chopped
75g butter, cubed
80ml beef jus, see Gusto Basics page 120

Potato galette

In a bowl place the diced onion and mix well with 2 tablespoons of cooking salt and leave for 1 hour.

In a saucepan place the cream, garlic, Dijon mustard, English mustard, thyme, bay leaves and butter. Bring up to a simmer and allow all flavours to infuse for 10 minutes. Strain and discard all the chunky bits. Season with a good pinch of sea salt and pepper.

After 1 hour squeeze all the moisture out of the onion with your hands and set aside.

Preheat oven to 175°C.

Generously butter a medium sized deep casserole dish.

Using a mandolin, slice the potatoes very finely. If you haven't got a mandolin use a sharp knife, slicing them as thinly as you can.

In a mixing bowl combine the sliced potato, cream and onion then layer the mixture in the casserole dish. Begin by putting a layer of potatoes on the bottom to form a base. In between each layer place a sprinkling of grated parmesan. Use your hands, making sure all the layers of potatoes are liberally covered in the cream mixture. Cover with greaseproof paper and bake at 175°C for 1 hour or until potatoes are soft and golden brown.

You can serve the potato galette straight from the oven, cutting each serve into squares or you can cool the galette and refrigerate for up to 2 days before use. This will present better than serving it straight from the oven, as it may break up a bit.

If you refrigerate the galette, cover and press down with a heavy weight overnight. Remove from casserole dish by gently turning upside down and easing the galette out. When required, cut into desired shape either with a knife or a large round pastry cutter and reheat on a tray at 250°C for 6–8 minutes.

Beef and mushrooms

Season steaks on both sides with sea salt and pepper and grill for 4–5 minutes on each side then leave to rest for 5 minutes.

While the beef is resting, sauté the mushrooms in some olive oil, adding the oyster mushrooms last as they do not require much cooking.

Add the thyme and season with sea salt and pepper. Remove from the heat and add a few knobs of butter so that it foams but does not burn.

Serve the steaks on top of a hot galette and spoon the mushrooms around the side. Drizzle with some hot beef jus.

Note: The above cooking time is for medium/rare. Cook longer for a well done steak.
Nathan

Butternut pumpkin tortellini, cherry tomato, sage butter

Serves 4 as a main course

Pasta
3 cups pasta flour
2 teaspoons salt
4 large eggs

Filling
1 butternut pumpkin
extra virgin olive oil
250g ground almonds
4 cloves garlic, crushed
100g grated parmesan cheese

Egg wash
1 egg, beaten

Sauce
150mls water
200g butter, knobs
1 punnet cherry tomatoes, halved
1 tablespoon sage, chopped
sea salt
freshly ground black pepper
200g rocket leaves for serving
parmesan wedge for shavings

Pasta

To make the pasta, mix the flour and salt on bench top and form into a mound.

Make a hole in the centre of the mound. Break the eggs into the flour and mix the dough until it is smooth and silky. Cover in plastic film and rest the dough in refrigerator for half an hour. You can use a dough hook in your mix master for this step if you have one.

Cut the dough into 4 pieces and flatten out and roll through a pasta machine. You will need to roll the pasta through the machine several times until you have thin sheets of pasta. Dust in between each sheet with flour to stop the sheets from sticking.

Filling

Preheat oven to 180°C.

Peel the pumpkin and cut into chunks and toss in olive oil. Place on a wire rack in a roasting tray, season with sea salt and cover with aluminium foil. Roast at 180°C for 45 minutes or until soft. Remove from oven and cool. When cool, place pumpkin in a clean tea towel and squeeze away all moisture.

In a mixing bowl break up pumpkin with a fork and mix together the ground almonds, garlic and grated parmesan.

Lay out a sheet of pasta on a lightly floured bench. Cut out circles with a large 8cm round pastry cutter. Place a heaped teaspoon of pumpkin filling in the centre of each circle. Brush the rim of each circle with egg wash. Fold over into a half moon shape. Seal by pinching and folding ends to make a parcel. You will need 8 tortellini per person for a main course or 4 for a starter.

Cook the tortellini in salted boiling water until 'al dente'.

For the sauce

Heat water in a large frying pan and when it comes to the boil whisk in the knobs of butter. Add the tomatoes and sage and season with sea salt and pepper.

When the tortellinis are cooked, drain immediately and add them to the pan of sauce. Turn off the heat making sure each tortellini is coated in sauce.

Serve with some rocket leaves and lots of parmesan shavings.

mains

Half a char grilled baby chicken, warm pea, artichoke and bacon salad
Serves 4

Marinade
2 x #1 spring chickens (split in half), ask butcher to butterfly or spatchcock them
1 lemon, zested
6 gloves garlic, grated
100ml extra virgin olive oil

Salad
8 small kipfler potatoes, peeled and boiled
extra virgin olive oil
4 artichoke hearts, quartered
4 rashers bacon, cut in strips
500g peas
100g baby spinach leaves
sea salt
freshly ground black pepper
Chicken salad dressing, see Gusto Basics page 120

Marinade
Marinate the chicken with the lemon zest, garlic and olive oil. Cover with plastic wrap and refrigerate overnight.

Preheat oven to 240°C.

Preheat a char grill or BBQ. Remove the chicken from marinade and grill for 3 minutes with the skin side down, making sure you get really good dark char marks. Transfer to oven and cook for a further 10 minutes until cooked all the way through. Insert a skewer into the thigh bone to ensure chicken is properly cooked and no blood appears.

Meanwhile prepare the salad.

Cut the precooked kipfler potatoes in half and sauté in a little olive oil until crispy and golden brown. Add the artichoke and cook until slightly coloured.

Separately fry the bacon strips until crisp and set aside with the potatoes and artichokes.

Blanch the peas in salted boiling water.

In a mixing bowl place potatoes, bacon, artichoke, peas and baby spinach leaves. Toss through with a good dash of olive oil, season with sea salt and pepper. Serve in the centre of a plate, drizzle the salad generously with dressing and the half chicken on top.

Note: This is a great dish for sharing. Rather than serving individually, place the salad on a large platter and place the half grilled chickens on top and pop it in the middle of the table and let guests help themselves. Nathan

mains

Pancetta, garlic, chilli and tomato spaghetti, Woodside goats curd
Serves 4 as a main course

400g spaghetti, bucatini no 6
extra virgin olive oil
200g pancetta, thinly sliced
1 red onion, finely diced
4 cloves garlic, crushed
1 hot red chilli, finely diced
1 punnet vine ripened cherry tomatoes, halved
2 tablespoons Italian flat leaf parsley, roughly chopped
4 tablespoons Woodside goat's curd

Cook the spaghetti in salted boiling water (with a dash of olive oil to prevent it sticking) until 'al dente' (check the packet for cooking time).

While the spaghetti is cooking, heat a large non-stick frying pan and add a good dash of olive oil. When the oil is hot, cook the pancetta until crispy, add the onion, garlic and chilli and cook until the onions are translucent. Be careful not to burn the garlic (turn the heat down a little if required).

Add the cherry tomatoes to the pan and continue to cook for a couple of minutes.

When the pasta is ready, drain it immediately and toss it in the pan with the other ingredients. Turn off the heat, add the parsley and season to taste. Add a little more olive oil if required. Serve immediately with a generous tablespoonful of Woodside goat's curd on top.

Note: Woodside goat's curd is available from good quality delicatessens. If you can't find it you can mix together equal quantities of mascarpone and goats cheese. Nathan

Chorizo, chilli and roast pepper fusilli

Serves 4

500g packet fusilli pasta
extra virgin olive oil
4 chorizo, sliced
1 red onion, finely diced
1 red hot chilli, finely diced
1 tablespoon baby capers, washed
100g green olives, pitted and roughly chopped
4 cloves garlic, sliced
80ml home made tomato sauce,
  see Gusto Basics page 123
2 red peppers, roasted, skin off, roughly chopped
150g parmesan cheese, grated
4 tablespoons chopped Italian flat leaf parsley
sea salt
freshly ground black pepper
parmesan cheese wedge for shaving

Cook the fusilli in a large pot of salted boiling water until 'al dente' (check packet for cooking time).

To make the sauce, heat a large non-stick frying pan and add a dash of olive oil. Sear the slices of chorizo then add the onion, chilli, capers, olives and garlic and sauté for a couple of minutes. Add the tomato sauce and peppers and cook a little longer until the sauce comes together.

When the fusilli is cooked, drain and add immediately to the sauce, tossing it thoroughly. Turn off the heat and add the grated parmesan and parsley. Check the seasoning and serve immediately with shavings of parmesan on top.

mains

Crispy skin salmon fillet with mash and pickled cucumber
Serves 4

potato mash, see Gusto Basics page 122
lemon butter sauce, see Gusto Basics page 121
extra virgin olive oil
4 x 200g Atlantic salmon fillets, skin on
sea salt
cucumber pickle, see Gusto Basics page 120 prepared 24 hours in advance
1 tablespoon dill, chopped finely

Prepare potato mash and lemon butter sauce. Start to cook salmon after the mash and sauce are ready (you can keep the mash warm on stove top) as the salmon cooks very quickly.

Heat a large non-stick frying pan and add a good dash of olive oil. Make sure the oil is really hot. Season the salmon generously with sea salt and place it in the pan skin side down for 1–2 minutes until crispy. Turn and cook for a further 2 minutes on the other side.

Remove the cucumber from the pickling juices and dress in olive oil and dill.

To serve, place a spoonful of piping hot mash in the centre of a serving plate. Spoon a generous amount of lemon butter sauce all over the potato. Place the cucumber pickle around the side and place the salmon on top.

Note: Not a meal to eat when on a diet (unless you're lucky enough to be on a high butter diet!). Nathan

Crispy duck salad with radicchio, beans and prunes

Serves 4

1 tea bag
20 prunes, pitted
4 large duck legs
1kg duck fat
75g walnuts
300g green beans
1 radicchio, picked
extra virgin olive oil
best quality aged balsamic

Infuse teabag in boiling water and soak the prunes in tea overnight.

Preheat oven to 180°C.

Place the duck legs in a deep roasting tray skin side up and cover with duck fat. Cover with aluminium foil and place in oven for 1–1½ hours or until the meat falls off the bone.

When the duck is ready remove from the fat using tongs and place on a wire rack in a clean roasting tray. Just before serving return the duck to the oven for 3–5 minutes until the skin is crispy.

Place the walnuts in a roasting tray and toast in the oven for 5 minutes. Place them in a clean tea towel and rub off the skins.

Meanwhile, wash and steam the green beans in salted boiling water and cook until 'al dente'.

Preheat a char grill. Brush the radicchio leaves with olive oil and char grill for 1 minute on either side.

Strain the prunes from tea and place in a mixing bowl with the walnuts, beans and radicchio leaves. Season with sea salt and pepper. Dress with olive oil and place on serving plate. Drizzle with aged balsamic and place a warm duck leg on top of salad.

mains

Prawn ravioli with leek and lemon butter sauce

Serves 4 as a main course

Pasta
3 cups pasta flour
2 teaspoons salt
4 large eggs

Filling
500g prawn meat, veined and finely chopped
4 cloves garlic, crushed
sea salt

Egg wash
1 egg beaten

Garnish
1 leek, washed and finely sliced
extra virgin olive oil
sea salt
freshly ground black pepper
1 tablespoon chopped Italian flat leaf parsley
200ml lemon butter sauce, see Gusto Basics page 121
4 Roma tomatoes, skinned, seeds removed and finely diced

Pasta
To make the pasta, mix the flour and salt on bench top and form into a mound. Make a hole in the centre of the mound. Break the eggs into the flour and mix the dough until it is smooth and silky. Cover in plastic film and rest the dough in refrigerator for ½ hour. You can use a dough hook in your Mixmaster for this step if you have one.

Cut the dough into 4 pieces and flatten out and roll through a pasta machine. You will need to roll through the machine several times until you have thin sheets of pasta. Dust in between each sheet with flour to stop the sheets from sticking.

Filling
In a mixing bowl, mix together prawn meat and garlic. Season with sea salt. Refrigerate until required.

Lay out a sheet of pasta on a lightly floured bench. Cut out circles with a large 8 cm round pastry cutter. Place a heaped teaspoon of prawn filling in the centre of each circle. Continue this process in neat rows, only putting filling in every alternate circle.

Brush the empty circles with egg wash and place on top of the filled circles. Pick up each ravioli with your fingers and very carefully seal the 2 circles by pinching together making sure you don't leave any air inside them. You will need 8 ravioli per person for a main course or 4 for a starter.

Cook the ravioli in salted boiling water for 4 minutes.

Garnish
Blanch the leeks in salted boiling water, drain and place in a bowl, add a dash of olive oil, sea salt, pepper and chopped parsley.

Present the ravioli in individual pasta bowls, sprinkle with diced tomato, lightly cover with the lemon butter sauce and place a tablespoonful of leeks in the centre of each.

Note: We've been serving this dish for years at Gusto. It is without a doubt our biggest seller and never leaves the menu. Kay

mains

Roast lamb rack with spinach, lentils and bacon, yoghurt dressing
Serves 4

4 x 250g lamb racks, frenched
sea salt
freshly ground black pepper
extra virgin olive oil
8 small kipfler potatoes, peeled and boiled
4 rashers bacon, cut into strips
200g baby spinach leaves
300g brown lentils, cooked
4 tablespoons salsa verde, see Gusto Basics page 123
yoghurt dressing, see Gusto Basics page 123
1 tablespoon sumac

Preheat oven to 250°C.

Season the lamb racks with sea salt and pepper and seal with a little olive oil in a hot, oven-proof frying pan fat side down. Transfer to oven and cook for 10–12 minutes. Remove from the oven and allow to rest for a further 5 minutes.

Meanwhile, cut the pre-cooked kipfler potatoes into barrel shapes and sauté in a little olive oil until crispy.

Separately, fry the bacon strips until crispy and set aside with the potatoes.

Whilst the lamb is resting, heat a non-stick frying pan and add a good dash of olive oil. Quickly sauté the spinach, add the lentils and then the crispy bacon and potatoes. Season with sea salt and pepper.

Turn off the heat and finish by stirring through the salsa verde to the pan. To serve, place lentil mixture in centre of plate with a lamb rack on top for each person. Drizzle with yoghurt dressing and sprinkle with sumac.

Note: The above cooking time is for pink lamb and the exact cooking time will depend on the size of the rack. Cook longer for well done. Nathan

mains

Roast Bangalow pork rack, creamy mash, braised baby gem, walnut, bacon and apple salad

Serves 4 as a main course

Bangalow pork rack, skin on (4 pin rack of pork)
sea salt
freshly ground black pepper
1 amount potato mash, see Gusto Basics page 122
4 tablespoons walnuts
4 rashers bacon, cut into strips
2 baby gem lettuces, washed, outer leaves discarded
2 granny smith apples, skin on, sliced
1 tablespoon chopped dill
lemon butter sauce, see Gusto Basics page 121

Preheat oven to 240°C.

Using a sharp knife, finely score the skin of the pork with a sharp knife (you can ask your butcher to do this). Rub the skin liberally with sea salt and place on a wire rack in a roasting tray. Roast for 1 hour or until the skin is crackling and golden brown. Insert a knife into the middle of the roast and check the knife is hot to touch. Remove from oven and allow to rest for 10 minutes.

Reheat potato mash in a saucepan with the lid on to keep warm.

Meanwhile, lightly toast the walnuts in a moderate oven for 5 minutes, remove and place in a clean tea towel and rub gently to remove the skins. Roughly chop.

Fry the bacon strips until crispy and set aside.

Blanch the baby gem leaves and the sliced apples in boiling water for 30 seconds to soften and place in a mixing bowl with the walnuts, bacon and dill. Season with sea salt and pepper. Lightly dress with a few tablespoons of lemon butter sauce.

To serve, carve the pork rack and serve one cutlet per person with a spoonful of mash and the salad to the side.

mains

Seared tuna spaghetti

Serves 4 as a main course

400g spaghetti, bucatini no 6
extra virgin olive oil
600g yellow fin tuna, 1cm sliced
sea salt
freshly ground black pepper
1 red onion, finely diced
1 red chilli, finely diced
60g artichoke hearts
1 tablespoon baby capers, washed
1 punnet vine ripened cherry tomatoes, quartered
4 cloves garlic, finely sliced
4 tablespoons chopped Italian flat leaf parsley

Cook the spaghetti in salted boiling water (with a dash of olive oil to prevent it sticking) until 'al dente' (check the packet for cooking time).

Meanwhile heat a large non-stick frying pan and add a good dash of olive oil. Season the tuna with sea salt and pepper and sear for 30 seconds only on each side. Remove from pan and set aside.

Clean the pan and add more olive oil, sauté the onion and chilli then add the artichoke, capers, cherry tomatoes and sliced garlic. Cook for 1 minute.

When the spaghetti is cooked, drain it immediately and add to the pan. Turn off the heat and return the tuna to the pan. Don't worry if it breaks up a little. Toss all the ingredients through the spaghetti, adding the parsley and a little more olive oil. Check the seasoning and serve immediately.

Note: Have all your ingredients chopped up and ready to go, so that you don't over cook this dish. Nathan

Bug linguine

Serves 4 as a main course

500g packet linguine
extra virgin olive oil
600g bug meat
1 red onion, finely diced
2 large hot red chillies, finely diced
4 cloves garlic, crushed
4 tablespoons Italian flat leaf parsley, chopped
2 vine tomatoes, peeled and finely diced
sea salt
freshly ground pepper

Cook the linguine in a large pot of salted water (with a dash of olive oil to prevent it sticking) until al dente (check packet for cooking time).

Meanwhile heat a large non-stick frying pan and add a good dash of olive oil. Wait until the oil is really hot and sauté the bug meat for 1–2 minutes, until it is slightly firm to touch.

Add the onion, chilli and garlic adding more olive oil if required. Be careful not to burn the garlic. Cook for a further minute. Turn off the heat, add the parsley and diced tomatoes.

When the linguine is cooked, drain it immediately and add to the pan. Add a little more olive oil, sea salt and pepper and toss all ingredients through the pasta. Serve immediately.

Clockwise from top left: surf lifesaver at main beach; Flat rock, Noosa National Park; Chris De Aboitiz with his dog riding the waves at First Point; checking the waves and dolphins at Boiling Pot; our favourite place for coffee after a swim at main beach in front of Sails Restaurant under the pandanus trees. Kay

the ocean

desserts

Most of the desserts at Gusto are old-fashioned favourites. They are very simply served with a scoop of home-made ice cream or a dollop of thick cream. No fancy patterns or tuiles on the dessert plate at Gusto. These desserts just taste good on their own. Nathan

- 98 Raspberry and white chocolate cheesecake
- 101 Apple tart tatin
- 102 Bread and butter pudding
- 105 Gusto lemon tart
- 106 Pistachio crème brulee
- 107 Strawberry Pavlova
- 108 Warm flourless chocolate cake
- 109 Warm raspberry frangipane tart
- 111 Rhubarb clafoutis
- 112 Warm soft-centred chocolate pudding with pistachio ice cream
- 114 Vanilla bean panna cotta and summer berries

desserts

Raspberry and white chocolate cheesecake
Serves 6

125g arrowroot biscuits
100g unsalted butter, melted
4 egg yolks
1 tablespoon water
110g castor sugar
150g white chocolate buttons
50ml pouring cream
150g cream cheese, brought to room temperature
450ml whipped cream
1 punnet raspberries, whole
raspberry coulis, see Gusto Basics page 123

In a food processor blitz the biscuits until they are a fine breadcrumb consistency.

Pour in the melted butter and mix through. Spoon 2 tablespoons of biscuits into 5cm round baking rings and push down into the bottom of ring to form the base.

Make a sabayon by placing the egg yolks, tablespoon water and sugar in a mixing bowl and whisk over a bain marie* for approximately 5 minutes. You will know it is ready when it holds a figure of 8. Remove from heat.

In a separate bowl melt the white chocolate and 50ml pouring cream over a bain marie. And in a separate bowl again soften the cream cheese over a bain marie.

Off the heat, mix together the cream cheese with the chocolate/cream mixture and then fold in the sabayon. Add the whipped cream, stirring gently until all ingredients are combined.

Pour on top of biscuit base, filling the rings right to the top. Refrigerate for at least 6 hours before serving.

When ready to serve, gently ease out of ring and neatly place whole raspberries on top. Drizzle serving plate and the berries with a little raspberry coulis.

Note: This cheesecake is also delicious with strawberries, simply replace raspberries with strawberries. The strawberries can be sliced and look attractive fanned across the top of cheesecake. Also use strawberries instead of raspberries for the coulis. Nathan

*A bain marie in this instance is a bowl (preferably stainless) that fits over a simmering pot of water, without the bowl touching the water. It is a gentle heating method as it only uses steam.

desserts

Apple tart tatin
Serves 6

6–8 large granny smith apples
1 litre water for poaching
250g castor sugar
1 packet of best quality rolled puff pastry sheets
vanilla bean ice cream for serving, see Gusto Basics page 123

Caramel
200g castor sugar
200ml water

Preheat oven to 250°C.

Peel, core and quarter apples. Place in a saucepan on the stove with water and sugar. Simmer until apples are slightly soft, set aside and chill until required.

Caramel
In a heavy based pan, heat the sugar and 100mls of water. When the caramel is dark golden brown, take off the heat and add in the remaining 100ml of water.

Pour one heaped tablespoon of caramel into each of 6 tart tins or blini pans about 10cm in diameter.

Lay apples in a fan formation on top of the caramel.

Cut a round of puff pastry for each pan and place on top of the apples and cook for 10–15 minutes or until golden brown.

Place a plate on top of the tart and quickly turn over the plate and remove tart tin allowing the caramel to ooze over the top of the apples. Serve immediately with vanilla bean ice cream and any remaining hot caramel drizzled over the ice-cream.

desserts

Bread and butter pudding
Serves 6

Bread and butter pudding
450ml cream
450ml milk
2 teaspoons vanilla essence
6 eggs
125g castor sugar
1½ loaves thinly sliced white bread
300g butter, melted
150g dried sultanas
150g dried apricots
150g dried figs

Crème anglaise
400ml cream
1 vanilla bean
4 egg yolks
75g sugar

For serving
Vanilla bean ice cream, see Gusto Basics page 123
6 large dried figs, soaked in hot sugar syrup for a couple of hours (optional), see Gusto Basics page 123

Preheat oven to 140°C.

Gently heat cream, milk and vanilla essence in a saucepan until warm but don't allow to boil.

In a mixing bowl whisk together the eggs and sugar.

Add the warm cream and milk into the egg and sugar mixture and whisk to combine and set aside whilst you prepare the bread and fruit.

Remove the crusts from the bread and cut each slice in half. Place the melted butter in a bowl and generously dip the bread in the butter.

Grease a deep baking dish with butter and start by layering the bread, followed by a sprinkle of sultanas, apricots and figs and repeat until all bread and fruit are finished. Pour over the cream and egg mixture and bake in the oven for 40 minutes until springy to touch and golden brown.

Crème anglaise
Gently heat the milk and vanilla bean in a saucepan on the stove, scrape out the seeds and put in the pod as well to infuse the flavour.

Whisk together the egg yolks and castor sugar and add to the warm milk, stirring continually with a wooden spoon until the sauce thickens and coats the back of spoon. Remove the vanilla pod and serve a generous amount of sauce with a slice of bread and butter pudding and a scoop of ice cream. Serve a large sugar syrup soaked fig on top of the ice cream.

Note: Use cheap white bread for this recipe as it soaks up the butter well and keeps the pudding nice and moist. Nathan

desserts

Gusto lemon tart
Serves 10

1 quantity of sweet pastry, see Gusto Basics page 123
450ml cream
9 lemons, zest and juice
13 eggs
585g castor sugar
100g castor sugar (to caramelise)
Clotted or double cream to serve

Preheat oven to 150°C.

Roll out sweet pastry about 5mm thick and line 28cm spring form tin.

Bake 'blind' for 10 minutes, take out of oven and cool on a wire rack.

In a heavy based saucepan heat the cream and zest of the lemon to infuse flavour but don't boil.

In a bowl, whisk together eggs and sugar until pale in colour and then add the lemon juice.

Pour the cream and zest into the mix and continue to whisk together.

Strain the entire mix through a fine sieve and leave to cool.

Skim off any froth from the lemon mix and pour into the blind baked pastry shell and cook for 45 minutes or until set.

Cool the tart on a wire rack.

When the tart is at room temp sprinkle the top with castor sugar and caramelise with a blow torch (if you don't have a blow torch you can heat the back of a large stainless spoon over a naked flame and lightly rub over the sugar).

Serve with clotted or double cream.

Pistachio crème brulee

Serves 12

20 egg yolks
400g castor sugar
1.8 litres cream
4 tablespoons pistachio paste
additional castor sugar to caramelise
pistachio biscuits, see Gusto Basics page 122

In a mixing bowl mix together the egg yolks and sugar until incorporated.

Place the cream in a saucepan and gently heat the cream, but do not boil.

Take the cream off the heat and add to the egg yolk and sugar mixture.

Put the mixture back on a low/medium heat and stir in a figure of 8 motion with a wooden spoon until the mixture starts to thicken slightly. Do not let it boil. It is ready when it coats the back of the wooden spoon.

Remove from the heat and stir through the pistachio paste. Strain through a fine sieve and pour into brulee moulds. Refrigerate for at least 6 hours before serving.

When ready to serve, sprinkle the top of each brulee with castor sugar and caramelise with a blowtorch.

Serve with pistachio biscuits if desired.

Note: Pistachio paste is available from good delicatessens. Nathan

desserts

Strawberry Pavlova
Serves 4–6

4 egg whites
240g fine castor sugar
1 tbsp cornflour
20ml white wine vinegar
greaseproof paper
2 punnets of strawberries
400g whipped cream
strawberry coulis, see Gusto Basics page 123

Preheat oven to 100°C.

Beat the egg whites in an electric mixer until soft peaks start to form. Gradually add the sugar, cornflour and a splash of vinegar, continue whisking until stiff and shiny (approximately 5 minutes).

Line a baking tray with greaseproof paper and dollop large spoonfuls of meringue leaving a couple of centimetres between each pavlova. Using the back of the spoon, make a small indentation on top of each pavlova to create space for the filling.

Bake for 1 hour then allow to cool on a wire rack.

Cut the strawberries into quarters and toss them in a bowl with a generous amount of coulis, making sure they are all nicely coated.

To serve, spoon a generous amount of whipped cream on top of each pavlova and put strawberries on top of cream allowing excess liquid to dribble over the sides.

desserts

Warm flourless chocolate cake
Serves 10

Greaseproof paper
150g chocolate
250g unsalted butter
8 eggs, separated
200g castor sugar
150g almond meal
½ tablespoon orange oil
1 tablespoon coco powder
fig ice cream for serving, see Gusto Basics page 120

Preheat oven to 170°C.

Grease with butter a 28cm spring form tin and line with greaseproof paper.

Place the chocolate and butter in a stainless steel mixing bowl and gently melt over a bain marie*. When melted remove from heat.

Separate the eggs and whisk the egg whites in an electric mixer until soft peaks appear, then add ½ the castor sugar (100g).

In a separate bowl whisk the egg yolks and remaining castor sugar (100g) with an electric mixer.

Stir the almond meal into the melted chocolate and butter until incorporated. While still stirring, add the orange oil and coco powder. Stir this through the egg yolk mixture and finally, fold in the whipped egg whites.

Pour the mixture into the greased and lined spring form tin and bake for 45 minutes.

Remove from tin and allow to cool slightly. Serve warm with fig ice cream.

*A bain marie in this instance is a bowl (preferably stainless steel) that fits over a simmering pot of water, without the bowl touching the water. It is a gentle heating method as it only uses steam.

Warm raspberry frangipane tart
Serves 10

1 quantity of sweet pastry, see Gusto Basics page 123
300g unsalted butter
150g castor sugar
150g icing sugar
6 eggs
1 tablespoon orange water
300g almond meal
60g plain flour
500g raspberries
icing sugar for dusting
clotted or double cream for serving

Preheat oven to 170°C.

Roll out sweet pastry about 5mm thick and line a 32cm fluted flan ring.

Blind bake for 10 minutes and take out of the oven and cool on a wire rack.

Meanwhile using an electric mixer, cream together the butter, castor sugar and icing sugar. Add the eggs, one at a time. Add the orange water.

Remove from mixer and stir in almond meal and flour. Pour into pastry case. Dot the raspberries neatly over the top of the tart.

Bake for 40 minutes until tart is set and light golden in colour.

Allow to cool slightly, dust lightly with icing sugar and serve warm with clotted cream.

Rhubarb clafoutis

Serves 6

Clafoutis
125g plain flour
50g castor sugar
3 eggs
300ml milk

Rhubarb
1kg rhubarb, washed
300g castor sugar
vanilla bean ice cream for serving, see Gusto Basics page 123

Clafoutis

Place all ingredients in a food processor and mix until well combined and of a batter like texture. Place in refrigerator and allow to rest for 1–2 hours.

Preheat oven to 200°C.

Wash and roughly chop the rhubarb and place in a large saucepan with the sugar. Stew on a low heat for approximately 20 minutes until the rhubarb is soft. Taste and add a little more sugar if required.

Thoroughly grease 6 blini pans or large ramekins with butter and pour batter three quarters of the way from the top. Spoon rhubarb on top of the batter and let it sink in. Keep any excess rhubarb for serving. Bake in oven for approximately 10 minutes or until set.

If using blini pan, remove clafoutis from pan and place on a serving plate. Warm up remaining rhubarb and spoon over the top. Serve with vanilla bean ice cream.

If using ramekins, leave in ramekin and serve remaining rhubarb on side with vanilla bean ice cream.

desserts

Warm soft-centred chocolate pudding with pistachio ice cream
Serves 6

Pistachio brittle
200g castor sugar
100ml water
100g shelled pistachio nuts

Chocolate puddings
clarified butter for greasing moulds, see Gusto Basics page 120
greaseproof paper
84g castor sugar
7 eggs
430g milk chocolate, buttons
250g unsalted butter
100g plain flour
pistachio ice cream, see Gusto Basics page 122

Pistachio brittle
Make a caramel by placing the castor sugar and water in a saucepan over low heat. Simmer, brushing the sides of the pan with cold water to prevent crystallisation until it turns dark brown in colour. Remove from heat and reserve a couple of tablespoonfuls of caramel to garnish the finished plate. Add the pistachio nuts to the remaining caramel.

Line a small baking tray with a sheet of greaseproof paper and pour the pistachio caramel on top. Spread it out evenly and place in the refrigerator until it goes hard.

When hard, blitz in a food processor until a rough powder. Store in an air tight container in the refrigerator until required.

Chocolate puddings
Preheat convection oven to 230°C.

Grease 6 stainless steel dariole moulds by brushing with clarified butter. (Dariole moulds are available from all good kitchen supply shops.)

Cut out 6 circles of greaseproof paper the exact size of base of moulds and place in the bottom of moulds.

In a mixing bowl whisk together the castor sugar and eggs until incorporated.

Gently melt the chocolate and butter over a bain marie*.

Pour the melted chocolate and butter into the egg mixture and mix together.

Sieve the flour and fold gently through the mixture. Now pour into dariole moulds, filling to 1cm below the top of the mould.

Bake in the oven for exactly 9 minutes.

To remove from the mould, run a knife gently around the sides of the pudding and ease the pudding gently out onto a plate. Remove greaseproof paper. Serve with a scoop of pistachio ice cream and sprinkle some pistachio brittle over the top of the ice cream. Swirl caramel around the plate.

A bain marie in this instance is a bowl (preferably stainless) that fits over a simmering pot of water, without the bowl touching the water. It is a gentle heating method as it only uses steam.

Note: Set a timer when baking the puddings because if cooked for any longer the puddings will not be soft in the middle. Ensure you use clarified butter to grease moulds, so the puddings retain their chocolate colour. Nathan

desserts

Vanilla bean panna cotta and summer berries
Serves 12

1500ml thickened cream
180g castor sugar
2 vanilla beans, scraped
2 leaves of gelatine, softened in water
40ml white rum
strawberry coulis, see Gusto Basics page 123
1 punnet strawberries, quartered
1 punnet blueberries, whole
1 punnet raspberries, whole

Put the cream and castor sugar into a saucepan. Scrape the seeds out of the vanilla beans into the pan and also put the whole vanilla beans into the pan. Place on a low heat and bring up to a gentle simmer for about 10 minutes.

Remove from the heat and add softened gelatine leaves until dissolved. Remove the vanilla beans.

Add rum and stir occasionally, allowing to cool slightly. Pour mixture into desired moulds and refrigerate to set for at least 6 hours.

Meanwhile prepare strawberry coulis.

To serve the panna cotta, submerge the mould quickly in hot water (without getting the mixture wet) and use a small knife to loosen and turn out onto a plate. Present the fruit around the panna cotta with a circle of coulis.

Note: Mangoes, when in season are a perfect partner to panna cotta. Simply cut a cheek from a ripe mango, sprinkle with castor sugar and caramelise using a blowtorch. Nathan

Surfing Tea Tree Bay, Noosa National Park

Gusto basics

120	Beef stock and beef jus	121	Seed mustard mayonnaise
120	Chicken salad dressing	121	Hot English mustard mayonnaise
120	Chicken stock	122	Octopus court bouillon
120	Clarified butter	122	Pedro ximenez dressing
120	Cucumber pickle	122	Pistachio biscuits
120	Dukkah	122	Pistachio ice cream
120	Fig ice cream	122	Potato gnocchi
121	Fish stock	122	Potato mash
121	Garlic dressing	123	Raspberry or strawberry coulis
121	Harissa paste	123	Salsa verde
121	Honey soy	123	Sugar syrup
121	Lemon butter sauce	123	Sweet pastry
121	Mayonnaise (base)	123	Tomato sauce
121	Harissa mayonnaise	123	Vanilla bean ice cream
121	Mustard and caper mayonnaise	123	Yoghurt dressing

terminology used in this book

Sweat   fry onion or garlic for a short time at medium heat until transparent.

Blitz   pulse on a high speed in blender or food processor.

Al dente   pasta or vegetable is still firm, but a knife slides through easily.

Cheek   cut fruits such as a lemon or mango vertically to expose the flesh either side of the seed or centre.

Season   add sea salt, pepper, lemon juice, sumac or our secret flavour – dukkah to enhance flavour.

Quenelle   form a neat spoonful using 2 spoons.

Cooking times are noted as guidelines.
All ovens are different and cuts of meat can be different thicknesses and textures. Please use your own judgment as to the length of time you prefer to cook a dish.

Gustobasics

Beef stock and beef jus

(makes about 5 litres of stock and 500ml of jus)

5 kg beef bones (ask butcher to saw bones into small pieces)
3 garlic heads
300g onions, chopped
300g carrots, chopped
4 bay leaves
½ bunch Italian flat leaf parsley
20g peppercorns

Preheat oven to 220°C.

Place bones on baking tray and roast for 30 minutes until bones are golden brown then add garlic, onions and carrots for another 10 minutes.

Remove bones and vegetables and put into a large stockpot with remaining ingredients.

Cover generously with cold water, bring to boil and simmer for 6–8 hours. Skim scum from top occasionally.

Strain and refrigerate.

To make beef jus, reduce the stock until it coats the back of a spoon.

Note that the reduced jus can be frozen.

Chicken salad dressing

(makes about 350ml)

2 egg yolks
½ tablespoon Dijon mustard
1 tablespoon capers, washed
2 tablespoons Italian flat leaf parsley, chopped
350ml vegetable oil
3 tablespoons lemon juice
sea salt
freshly ground black pepper
½ teaspoon harissa paste, see Gusto Basics page 121 (optional for a good kick)

Put egg yolks, Dijon mustard, capers and parsley in a food processor and whisk to combine. Slowly add a gentle stream of vegetable oil until all the oil is incorporated. Add the lemon juice and season with sea salt and pepper. Finally, add the harissa paste, adding more or less, depending how spicy you like it. Place in an airtight container and store in the refrigerator.

Note: If the dressing is a little thick, thin it down by whisking through a small amount of hot water. The harissa paste is optional, as is quite hot. Nathan

Chicken stock

(makes about 2 litres)

3 chicken carcasses
1 onion, chopped
1 carrot, chopped
1 stick celery, chopped
1 bay leaf
5 sprigs thyme
5 parsley stalks
6 black peppercorns

Place chicken carcasses in a large pot and cover generously with cold water. Add remaining ingredients and simmer for 4 hours. Check the stock every ½ hour to skim the scum off the top. Strain stock and chill. Remove fat that has risen and refrigerate. Keeps for 2–3 days in the fridge or it can be frozen.

Clarified butter

(makes about 200g)

250g butter

Gently heat the butter in a saucepan until melted. Refrigerate until solid. Discard the milky looking whey and keep the butter in container in the refrigerator.

Cucumber pickle

(makes a small tub)

250ml water
100ml white wine vinegar
125ml castor sugar
5 juniper berries
2 bay leaves
1 continental cucumber

Place the water, white wine vinegar, sugar, juniper berries and bay leaves in a saucepan and bring to the boil. As soon as the liquid boils remove the saucepan from the heat, cool and transfer to an airtight container and refrigerate.

Peel the cucumber and cut in half lengthways. Scrape out the seeds and slice into half moon shapes. Place the cucumber in the chilled pickling juices and leave overnight. The cucumber will keep for up to 3 days in the pickle.

Dukkah

(makes a small tub)

150g hazelnuts
5 tablespoons cumin seeds
5 tablespoons coriander seeds
1 teaspoon sea salt
20 tablespoons sesame seeds

Preheat oven to 160°C.

Place the hazelnuts in a roasting tray and roast for 5 minutes. Remove from oven, place in a clean tea towel and rub to remove the skins. Blitz in food processor until they are a fine consistency.

Place cumin and coriander seeds in a roasting tray and roast for 5 minutes. Remove from oven and grind in an electric spice grinder. Mix in the hazelnuts and sesame seeds. Store in an airtight container.

Note: This is a secret flavouring for salads and gives a great Moorish taste. Nathan

Fig ice cream

(makes about 1.5 litres)

Butterscotch
100g castor sugar
100ml water
100ml cream

Ice cream
175g dried figs, finely chopped
500ml milk
500ml cream
6 egg yolks
100g castor sugar
25g milk powder
75g dextrose

Butterscotch

In a heavy based pan, heat the sugar and 100mls of water. When the caramel is dark golden brown remove from heat and add the cream. Set aside.

Ice cream

Place the figs, milk and cream in a saucepan and warm to infuse flavours (do not boil). Take off heat.

Lightly whisk the egg yolks, castor sugar, milk powder and dextrose in a mixing bowl.

Whisk the 3 mixtures together and put in a clean saucepan. Bring up to a medium heat, stirring constantly with a wooden spoon until it reaches 80°C (use a thermometer; do not allow it to boil). Cool and refrigerate overnight.

Churn in an ice cream machine and store in the freezer.

Fish stock

(makes about 2 litres)

3 small fish, heads and bones only
2 litres cold water
1 onion, chopped
1 carrot, chopped
1 stick celery, chopped
2 bay leaves
5 parsley stalks
6 black peppercorns

Place the fish heads and bones in a large pot and cover generously with cold water. Add the remaining ingredients, bring to the boil and simmer for 20 minutes. Check the stock every few minutes and skim the scum off the top. Strain stock through a fine strainer or muslin. Refrigerate for up to 2 days.

Garlic dressing

(makes about 300ml)

2 egg yolks
½ tablespoon Dijon mustard
1 clove garlic, grated
25ml lemon juice
50g grated parmesan
300ml vegetable oil
sea salt

Put the egg yolks and Dijon mustard in a food processor and combine. Add the garlic, lemon juice and parmesan. Continue to whisk, adding a steady stream of oil until all the oil is incorporated. Season with sea salt to taste. If the dressing is a bit thick, thin it down by adding a small amount of hot water.

Harissa paste

(makes a small tub)

1 tablespoon cumin seeds
1 tablespoon coriander seeds
1 tablespoon caraway seeds
500g red chillies
3 garlic bulbs
2 lemons
5 tablespoons chopped mint
sea salt
freshly cracked pepper

Place seeds in a frying pan and heat until aromas are released, then remove from pan so they don't continue cooking, and cool.

Grind the seeds in a spice grinder until a fine powder.

Using a food processor or blender, blend all ingredients except mint into a pulp. Put mix in muslin and place in a strainer and allow liquid to drain, until the paste is just moist, and then mix mint through the paste.

Cover and refrigerate until ready to use.

Note: even a teaspoon of harissa paste gives dressings a real kick. Nathan

Honey soy

(makes 350ml)

250ml soy manis
100ml honey

Combine the two ingredients in a saucepan. Warm through on low heat and remove from heat.

Cool and refrigerate until required.

Lemon butter sauce

(makes about 250ml)

20mls lemon juice
20ml water
2 bay leaves
2 garlic cloves, peeled and finely chopped
250g butter, diced
sea salt

Put the lemon juice, water, bay leaves and garlic in a saucepan on high heat.

Turn down to medium heat and gradually add the diced butter, constantly whisking. As all the butter is added it will emulsify with the liquid creating a beautiful, rich sauce.

Strain and season with sea salt.

Mayonnaise

(makes about 500ml)

3 egg yolks
1 tablespoon Dijon mustard
sea salt
freshly ground black pepper
2 tablespoons lemon juice
500ml vegetable oil

Put egg yolks, Dijon mustard, pinch of sea salt and pepper in a bowl and whisk to combine.

Add a squeeze of lemon juice and vigorously whisk until the yolks start to thicken.

Continue to whisk adding a steady stream of oil until all the oil is incorporated. Check seasoning. Store in an airtight container in the refrigerator.

Note: If the mayonnaise is a little thick, thin it down by whisking through a small amount of hot water. Nathan

Harissa mayonnaise

For a spicy mayonnaise, whisk in 1 teaspoon of harissa paste to mayonnaise base, taste-testing to check how much spice you like. Add more if you like it hot, see Gusto Basics page 121.

Mustard and caper mayonnaise

For a mustard and caper mayonnaise, whisk in 2 tablespoons of Dijon mustard and 4 tablespoons of washed baby capers to the mayonnaise base.

Seed mustard mayonnaise

For a seed mustard mayonnaise, whisk in 2 tablespoons of seed mustard to the mayonnaise base.

Hot English mustard mayonnaise

For a hot English mustard mayonnaise, whisk in 4 tablespoons of English mustard to the mayonnaise base.

Gustobasics

Octopus court bouillon

(makes about 2 litres)

2 litres water
2 bay leaves
2 tablespoons sea salt
1 lemon

Bring the water to the boil with the bay leaves and salt. Cut the lemon in half and squeeze the juice into the pot. Also add the remainder of the lemon, skin and all.

Note: This is not a traditional court bouillon, we only use the above recipe for poaching our octopus. Nathan

Pedro ximenez dressing

(makes about 375ml)

30ml pedro ximenez sherry
30ml sherry vinegar
½ clove garlic, crushed
sea salt
freshly ground black pepper
½ teaspoon Dijon mustard
300ml extra virgin olive oil

In a mixing bowl whisk together pedro ximinez, sherry vinegar, garlic, pinch salt, black pepper and Dijon mustard. When ingredients are incorporated, slowly whisk in the olive oil. Check seasoning. Store in refrigerator.

Pistachio biscuits

(makes about 40–50 wafer thin biscuits)

3 egg whites
85g castor sugar
250g plain flour
125g pistachios, shelled
greaseproof paper
icing sugar for dusting

Preheat oven to 180°C.

Grease an 8cm x 25cm bar tin and line the base with baking paper.

Whisk egg whites and sugar. Gradually fold in flour and pistachios.

Spoon mixture into the tin and bake in oven for 40–45mins or until firm to touch. Remove from tin and allow to cool.

Lower oven temperature to 140°C. Using a very sharp bread knife slice thinly into wafers. Place wafers on a baking tray and return to oven for 3–5 minutes, until biscuits have crisped up. Store in an airtight container.

To serve, dust with icing sugar.

Note: Other nuts can be used in this recipe. Nathan

Pistachio ice cream

(makes about 1 litre)

50g pistachio nuts, shelled
½ tablespoon pistachio paste
500ml milk
500ml cream
6 egg yolks
100g castor sugar
25g milk powder
75g dextrose

Crush the pistachio nuts finely in a food processor.

Place the crushed pistachio nuts, pistachio paste, milk and cream in a saucepan and warm to infuse flavours (do not boil). Take off heat.

Lightly whisk the egg yolks, castor sugar, milk powder and dextrose in a mixing bowl.

Whisk the 2 mixtures together and place in a saucepan. Bring up to a medium heat, stirring constantly with a wooden spoon until it reaches 80°C (use a thermometer; do not allow it to boil). Cool and refrigerate overnight.

Churn in an ice cream machine and store in the freezer.

Potato gnocchi

(serves 6)

1.2kg desiree potatoes
3 egg yolks
120g parmesan, grated
sea salt
400g strong flour

Peel potatoes, then boil them until they are cooked right through. Strain and put back in the pot to remove excess water and steam. While the potatoes are still hot, pass through a mouli or a fine sieve.

Bring a large saucepan of salted water to the boil.

Place the mashed potato on a workbench and spread out. With your hands make a well in the centre. Add the egg yolks and parmesan and mix well. Add a good pinch of salt and flour and knead until a dough forms.

Divide the dough into quarters. Roll out each quarter into a long thin sausage shape, approximately 1cm in diameter and cut each sausage into 2.5cm lengths.

Drop the gnocchi in boiling water for a few minutes. The gnocchi is ready when the dumplings float to the top of the water.

Remove with a slotted spoon and drain on paper towel to remove excess water, and add to desired sauce.

Potato mash

(makes enough for 4–6)

1kg desiree potatoes, washed
175g butter
175ml milk
Sea salt

Peel potatoes and place in a pot and cover with water and add 1tablespoon salt to the water.

Cook potatoes until soft then strain. Return strained potatoes to the pot and gently heat while stirring with a wooden spoon, to evaporate any remaining water.

Pass potato through a mouli or a potato ricer while it is still hot.

Heat the milk and butter and add to the potato. Season to taste.

Note: In the restaurant I prepare the mash before service and re-heat it when needed. To make it nice and creamy I stir in a good splash of cream. If you do reheat your mash at home, make sure you stir it well to avoid lumps and make sure it is piping hot before serving. Nathan

Raspberry or strawberry coulis

(makes about 350mls)

100g castor sugar
250g raspberries or strawberries

Place the raspberries or strawberries in the blender with sugar and blend until a smooth consistency. Place in a squirt bottle and store in refrigerator.

Note, if using raspberries, strain through a fine sieve.

Salsa verde

(makes a small tub)

1 clove garlic, crushed
1 tablespoon mustard fruits, chopped
1 tablespoon capers, washed
½ small red onion diced
1 bunch Italian flat leaf parsley
150ml extra virgin olive oil
1 lemon, juice
sea salt
freshly ground black pepper

In a food processor pulse garlic, mustard fruit, capers, onion and parsley until combined.

Gradually add the olive oil and lemon juice. Season with sea salt and pepper.

Store in refrigerator but remove from fridge half an hour before use and stir well.

Sugar syrup

(makes 1 litre)

500g sugar
500ml water

Heat water and sugar in a saucepan until the sugar dissolves. Keep covered in the refrigerator.

Sweet pastry

(makes enough for large flan such as a 28cm spring form tin)

250g plain flour
100g pure icing sugar
100g unsalted butter, diced and hard
1 egg and 2 egg yolks

In a food processor place the flour, icing sugar and butter and pulse until breadcrumb consistency. Add 2 egg yolks and 1 whole egg and pulse to bring together. Wrap in plastic film and refrigerate for 1 hour.

Preheat oven to 180°C.

To roll out pastry, turn in quarterly rotations to maintain an even thickness and round shape. Roll the pastry on the back of your rolling pin to pick it up and place into required flan.

Line the pastry shell with plastic film and dry chick peas or baking beans. Bake for 10 mins at 180°C. Cool, remove plastic film and baking beans, and your tart is ready to fill.

Note: Baking paper can be substituted for plastic film. Nathan

Tomato sauce

(makes about 500ml)

extra virgin olive oil
½ onion, finely chopped
3 cloves garlic, crushed
1 400g can whole peeled tomatoes
sea salt
freshly ground black pepper

Heat a sauce pan and add a dash of olive oil. Sautee onions until transparent, add garlic and tomatoes. Simmer for 20 minutes.

Season with sea salt and pepper. Blitz in food processor, allow to cool and store in refrigerator until required.

Vanilla bean ice cream

(makes about 1 litre)

2 vanilla beans
500ml milk
500ml cream
6 egg yolks
100g castor sugar
25g milk powder
75g dextrose

Split the vanilla beans lengthways and scrape out the seeds. Place in a saucepan along with the beans, milk and cream and warm to infuse vanilla (do not boil). Take off the heat.

Lightly whisk the egg yolks, castor sugar, milk powder and dextrose in a mixing bowl.

Whisk the 2 mixtures together and put in a saucepan. Bring up to a medium heat, stirring constantly with a wooden spoon until it reaches 80°C (use a thermometer; do not allow it to boil). Strain the mixture and refrigerate overnight.

Churn in an ice cream machine and store in freezer.

Yoghurt dressing

(makes about 300ml)

250ml Greek yoghurt
20ml extra virgin olive oil
50ml honey
lemon juice to taste

Put the yoghurt in a bowl, whisk in olive oil, honey and season with a squeeze of lemon juice. Place in an airtight container and refrigerate until required.

index

starters

Asparagus, steamed, with fried duck egg, mustard and caper mayonnaise 41

Beans, steamed, with feta and dukkah 51

Beef carpaccio, anchovy and almond dressing 26

Beef salad, warm, with crispy potato cake, baby gem and walnut salad, mustard dressing 50

Broad bean, fennel and feta tart 57

Crab cakes, pea, fennel and feta salad 29

Duck spring rolls 36

Fish chowder 48

Garfish wrapped in vine leaves with salsa verde 32

Ham, Serrano, char grilled peach and blue cheese salad, pedro ximenez dressing 46

Mackerel, smoked warm tart, lyonnaise sauce 58

Meat board with peach chutney 38

Octopus, BBQ, pepper mousse, gremolata 23

Oysters with watermelon salsa and fresh lime 30

Pancetta wrapped figs with goats curd and walnut dressing 24

Pork, Bangalow, and pistachio terrine with prunes and watercress 20

Prawn and garlic bruschetta 42

Salad, baby gem, blue cheese and walnut 35

Salad, Greek 37

Salmon ceviche 25

Salmon gravalax, potato, caper and red onion salad 44

Salt cod brandade with grilled ciabatta, pear and watercress salad 27

Trout, smoked with pickled cucumber and potato salad 49

Tuna tartare, avocado puree 55

Zucchini flowers stuffed, tempura battered 52

mains

Beef, eye fillet with potato galette and mushrooms 74

Bug linguine 92

Butternut pumpkin tortellini, cherry tomato, sage butter 76

Chicken, baby, char grilled, with warm pea, artichoke and bacon salad 79

Chorizo, chilli and roast pepper fusilli 81

Duck salad with radicchio, beans and prunes 85

Lamb gnocchi, peas, mint, and Jerusalem artichoke chips 70

Lamb rack, roast with spinach, lentils and bacon, yoghurt dressing 88

Octopus and chorizo, BBQ, braised peppers and chickpeas 73

Pancetta, garlic, chilli and tomato spaghetti, Woodside goats curd 80

Prawn ravioli with leek and lemon butter sauce 86

Pork rack roast, creamy mash, braised baby gem, walnut, bacon and apple salad 91

Rabbit, braised 64

Salmon, crispy skin fillet, with mash and pickled cucumber 82

Spatchcock, BBQ, apple and raisin couscous 67

Tuna, seared with spaghetti 92

Veal fillets, BBQ with warm pumpkin, pine nut and goat's feta salad 68

desserts

Apple tart tatin 101

Bread and butter pudding 102

Cheesecake, raspberry and white chocolate 98

Chocolate cake, flourless 108

Chocolate pudding, soft centred with pistachio ice cream 112

Crème brulee, pistachio 106

Frangipane tart, raspberry 109

Lemon tart, Gusto 105

Pavlova, strawberry 107

Panna cotta, vanilla bean and summer berries 114

Rhubarb clafoutis 111

Gusto basics

Beef stock and beef jus 120

Chicken salad dressing 120

Chicken stock 120

Clarified butter 120

Cucumber pickle 120

Dukkah 120

Ice cream
    Fig 120
    Pistachio 122
    Vanilla bean 123

Fish stock 121

Garlic dressing 121

Harissa paste 121

Honey soy 121

Lemon butter sauce 121

Mayonnaise 121
    Harissa
    Hot English mustard
    Mustard and caper
    Seed mustard

Octopus court bouillon 122

Pedro ximenez dressing 122

Pistachio biscuits 122

Potato 122
    gnocchi
    mash

Coulis, raspberry or strawberry 123

Salsa verde 123

Sugar syrup 123

Pastry, sweet 123

Tomato sauce 123

Yoghurt dressing 123

The bronze statue of Harrold the koala guards the entrance to Noosa National Park at Little Cove. The best koala viewing is to be found in the tall trees at the entrance and as you walk along the Coastal track to Tea Tree Bay. Keep looking up! Look out for all the other native flora and fauna along the way. Kay

the park